Larkin Dunton

Methods of Teaching Arithmetic in Primary Schools

Larkin Dunton

Methods of Teaching Arithmetic in Primary Schools

ISBN/EAN: 9783337004880

Printed in Europe, USA, Canada, Australia, Japan

Cover: Foto ©Andreas Hilbeck / pixelio.de

More available books at **www.hansebooks.com**

METHODS

OF

TEACHING ARITHMETIC

IN

PRIMARY SCHOOLS

BY

LARKIN DUNTON, LL.D.

HEAD-MASTER OF THE BOSTON NORMAL SCHOOL

SILVER, BURDETT & CO., PUBLISHERS

NEW YORK ... BOSTON ... CHICAGO

1891

COPYRIGHT, 1887,
BY LARKIN DUNTON.

TYPOGRAPHY BY J. S. CUSHING & CO., BOSTON.
PRESSWORK BY BERWICK & SMITH, BOSTON.

PREFACE.

IT has long seemed to the author that there was needed in this country a manual for teachers, which should set forth, in systematic order and fully, the process of procedure on the part of the teacher in developing in the pupils ideas of numbers and their relations, ideas of numerical processes, and ideas of the signs by which both are represented. The present work is an attempt to supply that need in the case of teachers of primary schools.

For illustrations and method of treatment the author is mainly indebted to the work of A. Böhme, formerly a normal school teacher in Berlin, *Anleitung zum Unterricht im Rechnen*. But Böhme is not responsible for any of the statements made in this work; because such omissions, additions, and other changes have been made as seemed desirable in order to adapt the work to the needs of American schools. While portions of this work are free translations from Böhme, others are independent discussions.

The scope of the work and the arrangement of topics can be seen by a glance at the table of contents.

While frequent reference is made to *Arithmetic Charts* by the same author, the methods here described are not dependent upon any particular kind of apparatus, but are equally applicable, whatever may be the apparatus in use.

If, by the introduction of this manual, and of his *Arithmetic Charts*, the author shall have made the teaching of arithmetic easier for the teacher, and more educational for the pupil, his purpose in preparing them will have been accomplished.

BOSTON, Sept. 15, 1888.

CONTENTS.

CHAPTER I.

	PAGE
NUMBERS FROM ONE TO TEN	7
Counting	7
Apparatus for illustration	8
Use of apparatus in counting	11
Slate exercises in counting	14
Number pictures	17
Arithmetic charts	22
Separating numbers into two parts	24
Learning the use of figures	37
Written exercises in addition	38
Written exercises in subtraction	40
Combined addition and subtraction	42

CHAPTER II.

NUMBERS FROM ONE TO TWENTY	44
Counting	44
Separating numbers into two parts	47
Teaching numbers from 11 to 20	53

CHAPTER III.

NUMBERS FROM ONE TO ONE HUNDRED	61
Counting	61
Reading and writing numbers	65
Addition	67

	PAGE
Subtraction	75
Addition and subtraction	78
Multiplication	82
Teaching the multiplication table	83
Applying the table to written work	90
Constructing the table	94
Preparation for division	97
Division	99
Dividing by two	101
Dividing by three	110
Dividing by other numbers to ten	113
Practice work	114

CHAPTER IV.

NUMBERS FROM ONE TO ONE THOUSAND	117
Counting and writing	117
Addition	119
Subtraction	122
Multiplication	127
Division	132
Written and mental arithmetic	137

CHAPTER V.

HIGHER NUMBERS	141
Numeration	141
Addition	147
Subtraction	149
Multiplication	152
Division	157

TEACHING ARITHMETIC.

CHAPTER I.

NUMBERS FROM ONE TO TEN.

1. COUNTING.

INSTRUCTION in arithmetic should begin with counting, since this is the foundation of all arithmetical operations.

When children enter school, they can usually count a little, that is, they can distinguish a few numbers of similar things by the appropriate words. But it frequently happens that the children know words which stand for numbers, merely as a succession of sounds, without knowing what number of things one word or another signifies. The teacher should be careful not to mistake this mechanical knowledge of words for a real knowledge of numbers, or for the ability to count. In order to give the child a definite idea of the meaning of the number words which are already partly known to him, we should direct his attention to the objects around him, and teach him the words which express their numbers. Through conversation we may lead him to observe that there are in the room one door and another door, and thus to comprehend the expression that one door and one door are two doors. When the meaning of the word *two* is thus made clear, it may be applied to different objects in the room, as to two hands, two feet, two eyes, two ears, two windows, etc.

In this way we may lead the child to the comprehension and application of the words *one*, *two*, *three*, *four*, etc., to *ten*.

We should thus use concrete objects in making the child acquainted with numbers and the naming of numbers. Since clear and correct ideas are based upon perception alone, it is necessary to connect the exercises in number in the lower grades continually with concrete objects. In order to reach the proper result in the shortest time, it is desirable to have some simple apparatus, by means of which all the necessary observations can readily be made.

2. Apparatus for Illustration.

Pestalozzi furnished such an apparatus in his *table of units*. This consisted of a table containing ten rows of rectangles with ten rectangles in each row. In each rectangle in the first row was one line, in each rectangle of the second row were two lines, and so on to the tenth row, in each rectangle of which were ten lines.

Other machines for illustrating number-teaching have been devised, involving the same principle, and recognizing fully the necessity of observation, which have been improvements upon Pestalozzi's. One of these consists of a black wooden board, about twenty inches long and twenty inches wide, in which are bored a hundred holes, in ten rows of ten each, so arranged that there are ten horizontal and ten vertical rows. In addition to this board are one hundred buttons of white wood or bone, with stems that can be stuck in the holes. This has several advantages over the fixed table of Pestalozzi:

1. It allows each exercise to be observed alone;
2. The children can see the numbers produced;
3. They can themselves perform the exercises;
4. The things to be observed are objects, and consequently much better than any signs; 5. The number pictures (to be explained hereafter) can be formed. Besides, it is very handy, and the exercises to be shown can easily be observed by the children who sit in the farther part of the room.

Where such an apparatus is wanting, the teacher may use for the same purpose wooden pegs, bits of pasteboard, cubes, and the like. Mothers and nurses might do much to prepare the children for instruction and education in numbers, would they take occasion to have them count and compare, while at play with their little plates, soldiers, building blocks, etc. It is possible, even while the sole purpose is play, so to direct them as to do much to prepare them for instruction and for the development of their powers.

Another piece of apparatus is the numeral frame, one form of which is much used in this country. The best kind is composed of a wooden frame about four feet long and two feet wide, in which, running horizontally from end to end, are fastened ten brass or steel rods; on each of these rods are ten easily moved wooden balls about an inch and a half in diameter. The whole is supported at a convenient height by means of upright standards attached to bars running crosswise at the bottom. It is well to have the balls painted different colors, say three red ones at the left on each wire, then three yellow ones, and four green ones at the right; or, two and two, black, red, yellow, green, and white. One-half the frame should be covered with a board, so as to conceal all the balls that are not used in any example. This apparatus has some special advantages. It can be made to present many examples very readily, the balls can be seen across the room, and, by means of the different colors, the number of balls in sight on any wire can be readily determined, even by the farthest children.

The two pieces of apparatus just described may be united in one by boring holes for the buttons in the board used for a screen for the balls, as shown in the cut. This board may be made to perform still another office by ruling vertical and horizontal lines across it through the rows of holes, namely, the forming of number pictures, to be explained hereafter.

There are other ingeniously constructed machines for teaching the first steps in number; but generally the simplest form is the best. Perhaps for general use the numeral frame that I have just described is the most desirable.

3. Use of Apparatus in Counting.

However necessary real observation may be for the first steps in arithmetical instruction, and even in exercises introduced later, yet, ultimately, observation must be replaced by ideas; ideas in the mind must take the place of objects without. The child learns to walk, at first, with help, then independently; he learns to dispense with assistance gradually. So it is with the use of observation in arithmetical instruction.

It has already been explained how a child may be made to gain clear ideas of the fundamental numbers, that is, the numbers from one to ten. But the work thus begun may be completed and the ideas impressed upon the memory by means of the numeral frame, in the following manner; or, indeed, the very first instruction may be so given :

Move out one ball on the upper wire, and ask, "How many balls is that?" The answer should be given in a complete sentence, thus, "That is one ball." Move out two balls on the second wire, and to the question, "How many balls are there?" should the answer follow, "There are two balls." But if the child does not know the word *two*, the sentence must be given first by the teacher.

In the same way show the class all the numbers of balls from one to ten, and teach the sentences, in connection with the observation, "There is one ball," "There are two balls," and so on to, "There are ten balls." Let these sentences be clearly and distinctly pronounced, now by individuals, and now by the class in concert, while the teacher points successively to the different groups of balls. Finally, let the children use the pointer.

When these sentences have been learned as the expressions of the several facts, let them be abbreviated, thus:

1. One ball, two balls, etc., to ten balls.
2. One, two, three, etc., to ten.

Next, teach the following sentences in order, in connection with the use of the balls:

1. After one comes two, after two comes three, etc., to ten.
2. One and one are two, two and one are three, etc., to ten.

Although the last two sentences are not exactly counting, yet they are in place here, for they result immediately from the facts learned in counting.

Up to this point we have had the children speak the sentences in the order of the numbers, so as to accustom them to the counting of objects, and to the use of number words in their natural order; because counting is the foundation of all arithmetical operations. Now, however, exercises may be given out of their order, so that the pupils may be led to count any number of objects, as fingers, windows, etc., or to tell their number.

When the children have become proficient in designating any number of objects up to ten by the appropriate word, in telling what number comes after each number, and how many each number becomes when increased by one, they may then be taught to count backwards from ten to one. The proper order of the steps may be indicated as follows :

1. There are ten balls, there are nine balls, etc., to one.
2. Ten balls, nine balls, etc., to one.
3. Ten, nine, eight, etc., to one.
4. Before ten comes nine, before nine comes eight, etc., to one.
5. One from ten leaves nine, one from nine leaves eight, etc., to one.
6. Ten less one is nine, nine less one is eight, etc., to one.

The method is the same as in counting from one to ten. The numbers and their relations are to be suggested by the observation of the balls, as they are presented by the teacher.

4. Slate Exercises in Counting.

Many classes of beginners are so constituted that the pupils are not all of the same degree of advancement, so that they cannot properly be taught all together. When this is the case, we have little need to consider the question of slate exercises; for these are, at this stage of the work, merely makeshifts; and, however closely they may be connected with the objects to be observed, the real teaching of the numbers cannot be dispensed with. But when the class contains two or more divisions, then the teacher must provide suitable exercises to occupy the rest of the children while he is engaged in teaching one division. For this purpose he must make use of the blackboard. Of course, exercises in writing furnish abundant means for occupation, especially where reading and writing are taught together; but exercises should be devised which satisfy the aim of arithmetical instruction. All exercises designed simply to keep the children busy are an abomination. When slate exercises are introduced as a means of teaching counting, they should be closely connected with the objects to be observed by the children; so that the work done by them will be a means of fixing in their minds the ideas gained by the observation of the objects.

The children should not at this stage be made acquainted with figures, for they are not yet able to represent in their minds, by means of figures, what the figures signify, because figures are purely arbitrary signs, and not pictures of numbers, in which the children can again find the units which they signify. Written exercises in number must, therefore, at first, consist of representations of numbers of units.

To prepare the children for these exercises, the teacher should write upon the board the following, or similar groups of marks, while the children observe and count. The board upon which these groups are written should be ruled in squares of convenient size, so that each line, star, etc., will occupy one square.

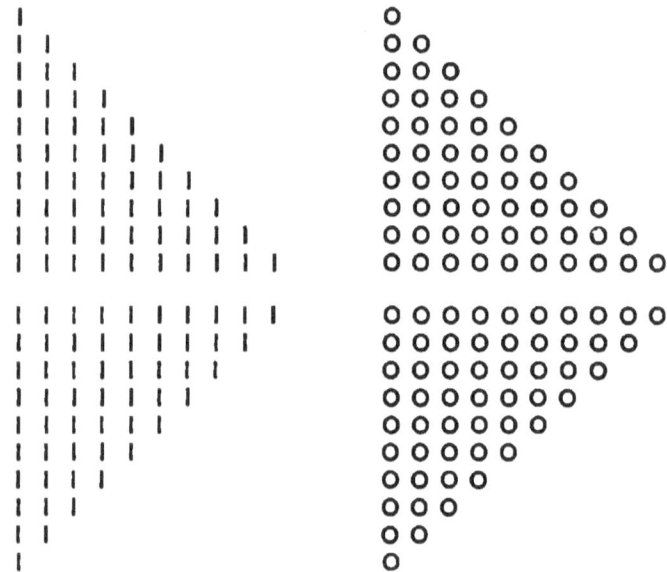

These groups may be formed of other figures, at the pleasure of the teacher; for example,

☐ ○ — + × T I.

The upper row of groups represents counting forwards, and each row of marks is one more than the row above; while the lower row of groups represents counting backwards, and each row of marks is one less than the row above.

The different lines, figures, etc., which the teacher can increase at his pleasure, serve both for a change, and for practice in writing and drawing. The slates should be ruled in squares corresponding with the ruling of the board; which may be done by scratching the slates lightly. This marking of the slates assists in establishing the habit of doing all work on the slate in an orderly manner. It is of much use a little later in fixing the habit of writing figures of uniform size, and in vertical and horizontal lines.

When the children have seen the groups formed, have counted the marks, compared and named them, so that their numbers are all well known, they may be required to copy them; and the closer they are required to follow the copy, the better, not only for the training of the eye and hand, but also for the arithmetic itself; for, as exactness in the order lightens the work of computing the numbers, so it makes clearer the knowledge of the relation of one number to another. Moreover, exactness here is of great moral value, inasmuch as it trains to habits of order and neatness.

Chart I. will now be found useful for review in counting and for copying.

5. Number Pictures.

Through the exercises already explained, the children may gain ideas of all the fundamental numbers, — that is, all the numbers from one to ten, — in their unity. The eye, however, is not in condition to see a large number of units lying side by side, or one above another, and grasp the units as a number.

The children, for the most part, have merely the power to count, — a power which is to be regarded only as the foundation. If a child is to obtain a total impression of a number at once, the number must be in the form of a definite picture, in which he discovers the number at a glance, and grasps it immediately in all its units. Such number pictures are presented at the bottom of Chart I.

CHART I.

For Review in Counting.

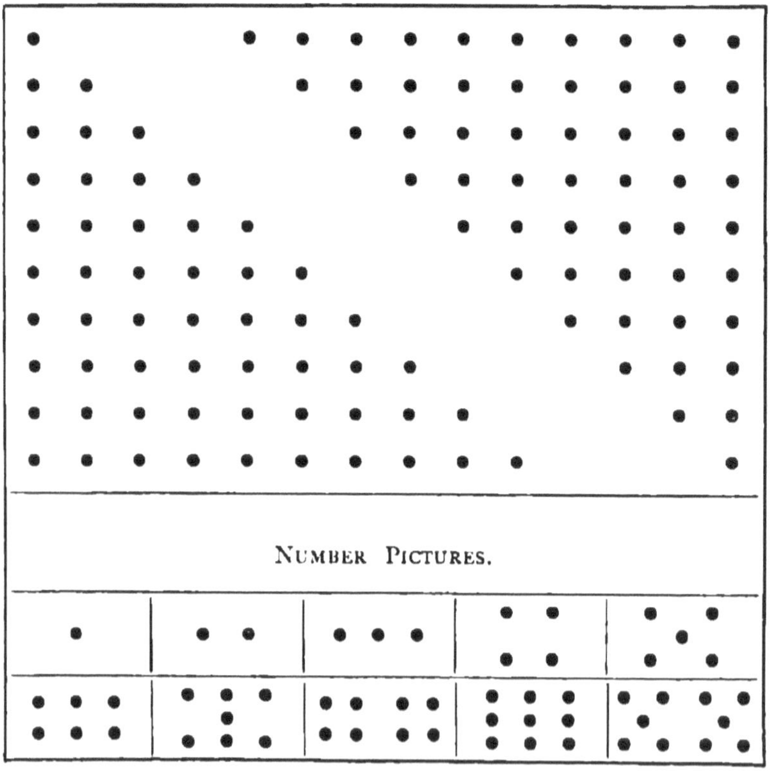

NUMBER PICTURES.

These rectangles with the enclosed dots should be put upon the board, one after another, and when they have been observed and the dots counted, they should be carefully copied on the slates, in order to impress them upon the eye and memory.

In regard to *one*, *two*, and *three*, there is nothing of importance to be said.

In *four* we see two points above and two points below; or two points at the right and two points at the left. Attention may be directed to the form of the picture by questions: "What do you see in four?" "Two points above and two points below." "What else?" "Two points at the right and two points at the left." But it will be taken for granted generally in this book, that the teacher knows how to develop the points of a lesson by proper questions, when they are suggested.

As the children copy, the arrangement of the dots makes clear to them the thoughts expressed by the following sentences, which may be developed by the proper questioning on the part of the teacher:

1. From four we can make two twos.
2. Two and two are four.
3. Four less two is two.
4. Two times two are four.
5. The half of four is two.
6. There are two twos in four.

In order to give further practice in the use of these sentences, refer to objects in which the number four appears; *e.g.*, a wagon has four wheels, two before and two behind; the cat, dog, mouse, etc., have each four feet; the table has four legs, etc.

Occasionally should practical problems be given: George has two cents, and gets two more; how many has he now? And so of the other relations of the numbers. But the use of these problems should not be carried too far, otherwise the arithmetical instruction lacks brevity and definiteness. I shall not introduce these problems often, because the live teacher can easily invent enough to fit the work upon the numbers, as they are studied, one after another; or, better yet, can find some good books of problems.

The number *five* may be produced from four by putting a dot in the midst of the four.

From *five* we can make four and one; it follows that

a. 4 and 1 are 5.   *c.* 5 less 1 is 4.
b. 1 and 4 are 5.   *d.* 5 less 4 is 1.

Six consists of two threes; it follows that

a. 3 and 3 are 6.   *c.* 2 times 3 are 6.
b. 6 less 3 is 3.   *d.* Half of 6 is 3.
  e. There are 2 threes in 6.

Furthermore,

f. 2 and 2 and 2 are 6.   *h.* The third of 6 is 2.
g. 3 times 2 are 6.   *i.* There are 3 twos in 6.
  j. 2 and 2 are 4; 4 and 2 are 6.

Seven consists of six and one, the one being in the middle; hence,

    a. 6 and 1 are 7.   *c.* 7 less 1 is 6.
    b. 1 and 6 are 7.   *d.* 7 less 6 is 1.

Eight consists of two fours; therefore

    a. 4 and 4 are 8.   *c.* 2 times 4 are 8.
    b. 8 less 4 is 4.   *d.* Half of 8 is 4.
        e. There are 2 fours in 8.

It is further obvious from the picture, that 2 and 2 and 2 and 2 are 8; or 4 times 2 are 8; the fourth of 8 is 2; and there are 4 twos in 8.

If the children are old enough and advanced enough to make it easy for them to comprehend, the following facts may be taught:

$\frac{1}{4}$ of 8 is 2,   If 1 apple costs 2 cents,
$\frac{2}{4}$ of 8 are 4,   2 apples cost 4 cents,
$\frac{3}{4}$ of 8 are 6,   3 apples cost 6 cents,
$\frac{4}{4}$ of 8 are 8.   4 apples cost 8 cents.
$\frac{1}{4}$ of 8 away, 6 is left,   If 1 orange costs 8 cents,
$\frac{2}{4}$ of 8 away, 4 is left, $\frac{1}{2}$ orange costs 4 cents,
$\frac{3}{4}$ of 8 away, 2 is left, $\frac{1}{4}$ orange costs 2 cents,
$\frac{4}{4}$ of 8 away, 0 is left. $\frac{3}{4}$ orange cost 6 cents.

Nine consists of three threes; therefore

    a. 3 and 3 and 3 are 9.   *d.* 9 less 6 is 3.
    b. 3 times 3 are 9.   *e.* 6 and 3 are 9.
    c. 9 less 3 is 6.   *f.* A third of 9 is 3, etc.

Ten consists of two fives; therefore,

    a. 5 and 5 are 10.   *c.* 10 less 5 is 5.
    b. 2 times 5 are 10.   *d.* Half of 10 is 5.
          e. There are 2 fives in 10.

While the teacher is instructing the children in these numbers, he must be careful, both in the oral and written work, to make them able to name the number pictures as soon as they are seen, and also to construct them on the numeral frame, or draw them on the board.

An excellent practice in comparing numbers grows out of forming one number from another. For example, put the number picture for five on the board, then ask, What must be done in order to make a seven? Must something be added, or taken away? How many must be added? Where must the dots be put? Again, How can seven be made from nine? etc. In all such cases, one number picture is to be changed to another by either addition or subtraction of the proper dots. Exercises of this kind are very useful; they exercise the children in the comparison of numbers, and prepare them for the division of numbers, which is about to be explained in detail.

6. Arithmetic Charts.

In addition to the apparatus for developing ideas of number, which has been already described, a few arithmetic charts will be found very helpful for reviews at every stage of elementary instruction in arithmetic. The author of this book has arranged a series of thirteen such charts, which are published by Silver, Burdett & Co. Miniature copies of them will be printed in this book, as they are needed for illustration; and they will be referred to simply by their numbers. Where they are not furnished to schools, teachers can put them on the blackboard, or on large sheets of paper, and thus save themselves much labor.

A word in regard to the use of the charts. The children should see each number and each exercise produced; that is, each illustration of a number, or of a numerical operation, should be made by the teacher, either upon the numeral frame, or upon the board, or with objects, just when it is needed to make the truth clear to the class. Hence all ready-made charts, or other illustrations, are to be used later, after this preliminary, but fundamental work has been done. They are to serve as a means for review and practice in what has already been made clear to the understanding.

The charts representing matter for observation are to be read forwards, backwards, vertically, and horizontally. The special use to be made of the different charts will be explained as they are introduced. In general, they are designed to lighten the labor of the teacher, while making the instruction more thorough and systematic.

7. Separating Numbers into Two Parts.

Upon a pupil's facility in the use of numbers below ten depends his progress in mastering numbers above ten. The greater his facility in the use of small numbers, if it is founded upon clear understanding, the surer and more rapid will be his progress in larger numbers. In order to attain this facility depending upon understanding, we must have the numbers regarded from as many sides as possible; this comes from the division, or separation, of the numbers into their component parts. From this division we obtain results for all the different fundamental operations in arithmetic, which are the more easily committed to memory, because they are all grounded upon a single result, namely, that of division. The results, however, which are obtained from this division, must, by no means, be learned by heart, as one commits to memory vocabularies or verses; they must become things of the memory through an unlimited amount of reckoning, — through practice. It is sufficient, at first, that a child, if he is to unite, for example, five and three into a single number, adds first one to five, then another, and still another, even if he represents the process to his senses by means of marks, fingers, etc.; yet continued practice must bring him to the point where the union of three and five in eight is a simple conception, a thing of the memory. If the child constantly perceives the three units in three, he will, in time, be able to unite three to five at once. We shall be able to bring him to this state of mind the more easily if we show him that eight consists of a five and a three. When, however, we have shown him this, he will be able, from the single observation, to understand the following four sentences :

    a. Three and five make eight.
    b. Five and three make eight.
    c. Three from eight leaves five.
    d. Five from eight leaves three.

If now, we use these sentences as the expressions for the truths which constantly appear before the eyes of the child, the results will finally become impressed upon his memory. This result will, of course, be reached in the case of some children quicker than with others.

Out of the above division we obtain two results in addition and two in subtraction. Another example will show that in a single division all the four fundamental operations of arithmetic may be illustrated. Out of eight we can make two fours. It follows that

    a. 4 and 4 are 8.   *c.* 8 less 4 is 4.
    b. 2 times 4 are 8.   *d.* The half of 8 is 4.
        e. There are 2 fours in 8.

In the first stages of arithmetical work, where the numbers are small, and the results to be gained through division are correspondingly few, the direct observation may result in clear mental pictures, or ideas. Here the connection between the various ground operations of arithmetic is so obvious from the observation, that it seems unnecessary to separate the treatment of the different operations. Hence, in this and the following stage, that is, in the treatment of numbers from one to ten, and from ten to twenty, the four fundamental operations may be united. All the different results are obtained because *every number below ten is divided into every two parts of which it is composed,* in the way shown in Chart II.

CHART II.

UNITING AND SEPARATING NUMBERS FROM TWO TO TEN.

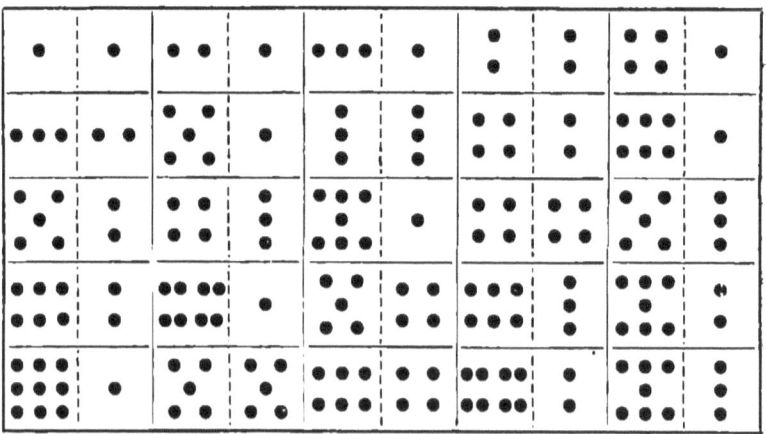

I will now give an explanation of Charts I. and II. and their use.

The upper part of Chart I. is for review work in counting. The dots may be counted under the direction of the teacher; and then they may be copied on the slates. During the work of copying, the children should always count the dots as they make them.

The lower part of Chart I. contains the number pictures from one to ten. These pictures are designed to furnish a means of impressing the ideas of the fundamental numbers, — that is, the numbers from one to ten, — upon the mind in such a way that they may reappear in the imagination of the pupil whenever needed.

These pictures should not be used as the sole means of developing ideas of numbers, but rather as a means of thorough review and impression. Figures should not be taught in connection with these pictures. The whole attention of the pupil should be given to the numbers and their production; mere figures will be prominent enough in his work by and by, however much pains may be taken to avoid it.

Chart II. is to show the parts of numbers to ten. Each number picture is to be formed at first by the teacher on the numeral frame, the blackboard, or other apparatus; so that the attention of the children can be directed to only one number. All the special facts in regard to the composition of the number, and the relation of its parts, are to be developed by proper questions, and by pointing to the parts to be seen.

As fast as the number pictures have been treated in this way they may be copied from the chart, and thus much labor on the part of the teacher may be saved. After, for example, the number two has been treated as indicated below, the first rectangle may be copied by the children. By this means the truths will be further impressed upon the mind. The teacher, however, should be sure that the children connect the proper name of the number, and the names of the parts, with what they write; so that numbers and names will become thoroughly associated in their minds.

THE NUMBER TWO.

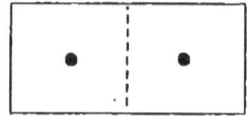

This is the first rectangle on Chart II. It shows that the number *two* can be divided into two units; hence the truth of the following sentences:

    a. 1 and 1 are 2.   *c.* 2 less 1 is 1.
    b. 2 times 1 are 2.   *d.* ½ of 2 is 1.
          e. 1 in 2 two times.

THE NUMBER THREE.

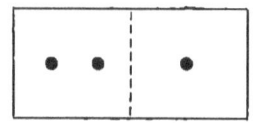

From three we can make a two and a one; it follows that

    a. 2 and 1 are 3.   *c.* 3 less 1 is 2.
    b. 1 and 2 are 3.   *d.* 3 less 2 is 1.

SEPARATING NUMBERS INTO TWO PARTS.

THE NUMBER FOUR.

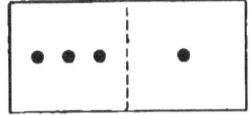 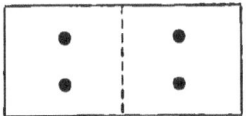

Four may be divided into: A. Three and one. B. Two and two. It follows that

A. a. 3 + 1 = 4.
    b. 1 + 3 = 4.
    c. 4 − 1 = 3.
    d. 4 − 3 = 1.

B. a. 2 + 2 = 4.
    b. 4 − 2 = 2.
    c. 2 × 2 = 4.
    d. ½ of 4 = 2.
    e. 2 in 4 = 2 times.

THE NUMBER FIVE.

 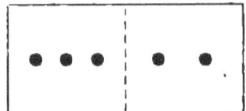

This may be separated into: A. Four and one. B. Three and two. It follows that

A. a. 4 + 1 = 5.
    b. 1 + 4 = 5.
    c. 5 − 1 = 4.
    d. 5 − 4 = 1.

B. a. 3 + 2 = 5.
    b. 2 + 3 = 5.
    c. 5 − 2 = 3.
    d. 5 − 3 = 2.

THE NUMBER SIX.

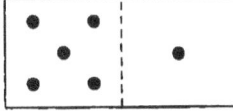 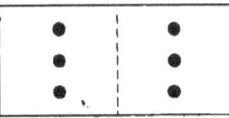 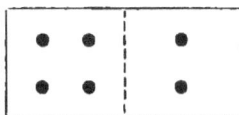

Six may be divided as follows :

A. Five and one.
a. $5 + 1 = 6$.
b. $1 + 5 = 6$.
c. $6 - 1 = 5$.
d. $6 - 5 = 1$.

B. Three and three.
a. $3 + 3 = 6$.
b. $6 - 3 = 3$.
c. $2 \times 3 = 6$.
d. $3 \times 2 = 6$.
e. $\frac{1}{2}$ of $6 = 3$.
f. $\frac{1}{3}$ of $6 = 2$.

C. Four and two.
a. $4 + 2 = 6$.
b. $2 + 4 = 6$.
c. $6 - 2 = 4$.
d. $6 - 4 = 2$.
e. $3 \times 2 = 6$.
f. $\frac{1}{3}$ of $6 = 2$.

THE NUMBER SEVEN.

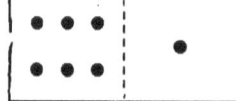 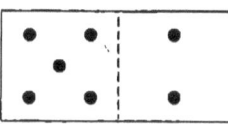 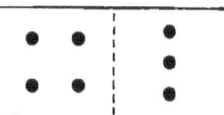

Seven may be divided into :

A. Six and one.
a. $6 + 1 = 7$.
b. $1 + 6 = 7$.
c. $7 - 1 = 6$.
d. $7 - 6 = 1$.

B. Five and two.
a. $5 + 2 = 7$.
b. $2 + 5 = 7$.
c. $7 - 2 = 5$.
d. $7 - 5 = 2$.

C. Four and three.
a. $4 + 3 = 7$.
b. $3 + 4 = 7$.
c. $7 - 3 = 4$.
d. $7 - 4 = 3$.

THE NUMBER EIGHT.

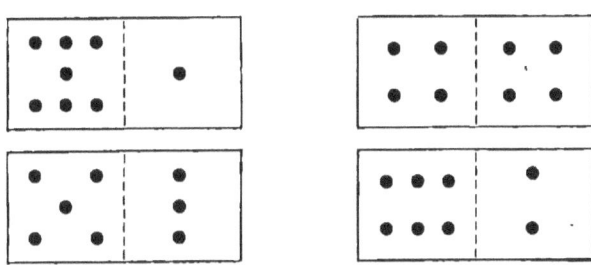

Eight may be divided into:

A. Seven and one.
a. $7 + 1 = 8$. c. $8 - 1 = 7$.
b. $1 + 7 = 8$. d. $8 - 7 = 1$.

B. Four and four.
a. $4 + 4 = 8$. c. $2 \times 4 = 8$. e. $4 \times 2 = 8$.
b. $8 - 4 = 4$. d. $\frac{1}{2}$ of $8 = 4$. f. $\frac{1}{4}$ of $8 = 2$.

C. Five and three.
a. $5 + 3 = 8$. c. $8 - 3 = 5$.
b. $3 + 5 = 8$. d. $8 - 5 = 3$.

D. Six and two.
a. $6 + 2 = 8$. c. $8 - 2 = 6$.
b. $2 + 6 = 8$. d. $8 - 6 = 2$.

THE NUMBER NINE.

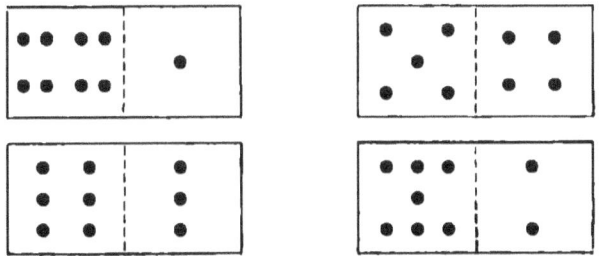

Nine may be divided into:

A. Eight and one.

a. $8 + 1 = 9.$ *c.* $9 - 1 = 8.$
b. $1 + 8 = 9.$ *d.* $9 - 8 = 1.$

B. Five and four.

a. $5 + 4 = 9.$ *c.* $9 - 4 = 5.$
b. $4 + 5 = 9.$ *d.* $9 - 5 = 4.$

C. Six and three.

a. $6 + 3 = 9.$ *d.* $9 - 6 = 3.$
b. $3 + 6 = 9.$ *e.* $3 \times 3 = 9.$
c. $9 - 3 = 6.$ *f.* $\frac{1}{3}$ of $9 = 3.$

D. Seven and two.

a. $7 + 2 = 9.$ *c.* $9 - 2 = 7.$
b. $2 + 7 = 9.$ *d.* $9 - 7 = 2.$

THE NUMBER TEN.

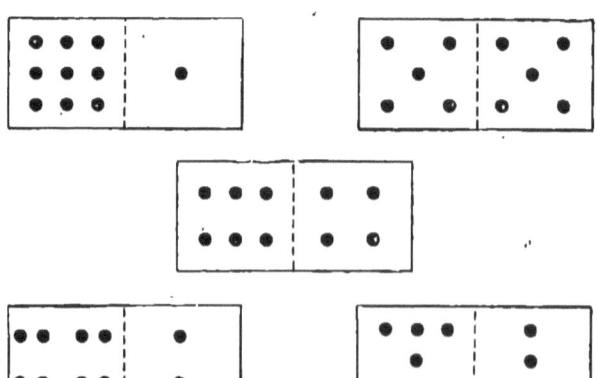

SEPARATING NUMBERS INTO TWO PARTS. 33

Ten may be divided into:

A. Nine and one.
a. 9 + 1 = 10.   *c.* 10 − 1 = 9.
b. 1 + 9 = 10.   *d.* 10 − 9 = 1.

B. Five and five.
a. 5 + 5 = 10.   *c.* 2 × 5 = 10.
b. 10 − 5 = 5.   *d.* ½ of 10 = 5.

C. Six and four.
a. 6 + 4 = 10.   *c.* 10 − 4 = 6.
b. 4 + 6 = 10.   *d.* 10 − 6 = 4.

D. Eight and two.
a. 8 + 2 = 10.   *d.* 10 − 8 = 2.
b. 2 + 8 = 10.   *e.* 5 × 2 = 10.
c. 10 − 2 = 8.   *f.* ⅕ of 10 = 2.

E. Seven and three.
a. 7 + 3 = 10.   *c.* 10 − 3 = 7.
b. 3 + 7 = 10.   *d.* 10 − 7 = 3.

FURTHER USE OF CHART II.

For further instruction in regard to the use that can be made of Chart II., I will explain some additional work upon the number eight. Arrange eight balls on the numeral frame, as shown below.

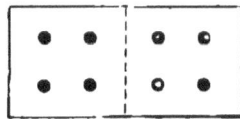

There are four balls at the left and four balls at the right; or, there are four balls above and four balls below. So, 4 and 4 are 8. Four balls are to be seen two times; therefore, 2 times 4 balls are equal to 8 balls. Two balls appear always under two other balls; hence $4 \times 2 = 8$.

If we take four balls from the eight balls, then four balls remain: hence $8 - 4 = 4$. This removal may be indicated by covering part of the balls. The line across the rectangle divides the dots into two equal parts. This may be shown on the frame by holding a pointer between the two fours. It follows that the half of 8 is four. Two balls appear four times; therefore the fourth part, or a fourth, of eight is two.

These considerations prepare for the following questions: How many are $4 + 4$? 2×4? 4×2? $8 - 4$? $\frac{1}{2}$ of 8? $\frac{1}{4}$ of 8? What number must one put with 4 to make eight? How many more is 8 than 4? How many less than 8 is 4? How many times 4 is 8? How many times 2 is 8? Of what number is 4 the half? Of what number is 2 the fourth? What part of 8 is 4? What part of 8 is 2? How many is 8 less 2×2? How many is 8 less 3×2? How many times 2 is 8 less 4? etc.

These exercises with pure numbers are the proper preparation for such simple practical examples as these: Charles has 4 cents, and Fred has 4 cents; how many have they together? Charles has 8 cents, and gives 4 of them to Fred; how many has Charles left? Charles got 4 cents yesterday, and 4 more to-day; how many times 4 cents has he? How many cents in all? Charles had 8 cents, and lost half of them; how many has he now? Charles and Fred together had 8 apples, and divided them so that each had an equal number; how many did each then have? Each of 4 children had 2 pears; how many had they all together? Four children divide 8 apples equally among them; how many does each receive? — Give a boy 8 pencils, and let him give one each to 4 other boys, and then one more to each of them. What is $\frac{1}{4}$ of 8? — One apple costs 2 cents; how many cents do 2 apples cost? 3 apples? 4? A yard of ribbon costs 8 cents; how much does half a yard cost? A fourth? Three-fourths? etc., etc.

In giving practicable problems it is often necessary to mention coins, measures, and weights. These should not only be well known, but they should often be shown to the children. The teacher should limit his problems to those coins, weights, and measures that are accessible to the children in their ordinary intercourse. The copper, nickel, and smaller silver coins are all the coins that should be mentioned in these early problems; the measures should be limited to the inch, foot, yard, pint, and quart; and the ounce and pound weights are enough. It is well to have all the measures involved in the problems given, constantly before the eyes of the children, so that they will be impressed upon the memory. As the work in numbers progresses, these illustrations may be enlarged. Their application will be indicated as we progress.

The number pictures which are studied with the children during the lesson should be copied upon the slates as written work. The teacher can at first make them upon the board, and subsequently have them copied from Chart II. When this has been repeated sufficiently, they may be written from memory.

The chart will also serve a good purpose in conducting reviews. What is represented in the chart may be expressed in words. In addition, the verbal expressions would run thus:

One and one are two.	Four and one are five.
Two and one are three.	Three and two are five.
Three and one are four.	Five and one are six.
Two and two are four.	Etc., etc.

This order from left to right on the chart is to be interchanged with the movement from right to left, from top to bottom, from bottom to top, and with exercises out of order.

By regarding each picture as a number, and covering first the dots at the right and then those at the left, numerous exercises in subtraction may be formed.

By means of these exercises all the facts of the addition, subtraction, multiplication, and division tables may be learned, where the sum, minuend, product, or dividend does not exceed ten. Since these results are of the greatest use in all arithmetical operations, they must be firmly fixed in the memory. This is to be done, however, by observing and stating the facts as shown on the chart, by copying the number pictures, and by written representations in figures, not by learning the statements, as such, by heart.

8. LEARNING THE USE OF FIGURES.

The ground already covered is sufficient for a fourth of a year, and, under some conditions, for a longer time. Hitherto the children have learned only from observation; now, however, they may without danger pass from things to signs, from numbers to figures. This transition may be made by means of the following chart:

CHART III.

USE OF FIGURES.

•	1	••	2	•••	3	•• ••	4	•• • ••	5
••• •••	6	••• • •••	7	•• •• •• ••	8	••• ••• •••	9	•• •• •• •• ••	10

| WRITTEN FIGURES. ||||||||||

•	1	••	2	•••	3	•• ••	4	•• • ••	5
••• •••	6	••• • •••	7	•• •• •• ••	8	••• ••• •••	9	•• •• •• •• ••	10

Through diligent copying, pointing, and reciting, the children will impress these forms upon the mind so that they can be made without a copy.

The different rectangles of Chart II. may then be copied, and with them the corresponding figures may be copied in similar rectangles, as follows:

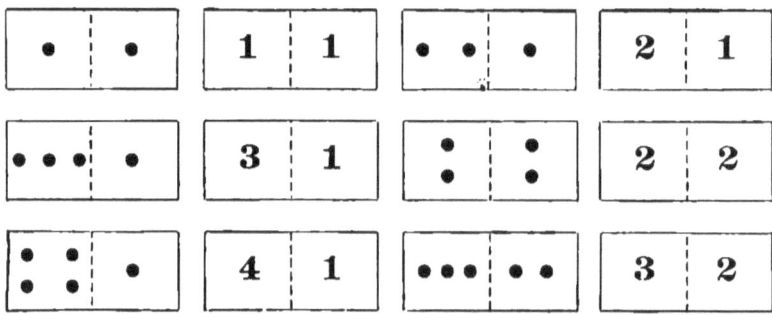

The rest of the chart may be treated in the same way.

9. Written Exercises in Addition.

In order still further to represent in figures the results gained through the preceding instruction, we make use again of Chart II., at first for the purpose of addition. The children must now learn the sign of addition (+, plus, or and) and also the sign of equality (=, is, or are). Then, by writing the figures for the dots seen in the different rectangles, they can form these series of numbers on their slates:

1 + 1 = 2, or 1 + 1 = 2.   3 + 2 = 5, or 2 + 3 = 5.
2 + 1 = 3, or 1 + 2 = 3.   5 + 1 = 6, or 1 + 5 = 6.
3 + 1 = 4, or 1 + 3 = 4.   3 + 3 = 6, or 3 + 3 = 6.

WRITTEN EXERCISES IN ADDITION. 39

2 + 2 = 4, or 2 + 2 = 4.   4 + 2 = 6, or 2 + 4 = 6.
4 + 1 = 5, or 1 + 4 = 5.   etc.   etc.

At first the work may be confined to a few of the number pictures, but it should be extended gradually till the whole chart can be represented in figures.

In order to teach regularity and order in the arrangement of the figures, it is worth while to have the slates ruled upon one side in squares of about three-eighths of an inch; the other side may be ruled in lines for writing. After the first year the squares may be omitted, but at first they are very helpful. A portion of the blackboard should be ruled in the same way.

When Chart II. can be readily interpreted in this way by figures, the reverse process should be introduced. The children should be required to translate figures into numbers. The teacher will write upon the board, for example, 3 + 2 = 5, and the children will copy the same, and then add the corresponding number pictures, thus:

$$3 + 2 = 5.$$

For a review, and for drill in this work, the upper part of Chart IV. furnishes a convenient means.

CHART IV.

Written Representation of Chart II.

$1+1=2$	$3+2$	$5+2$	$6+2$	$9+1$
$2+1=$	$5+1$	$4+3$	$8+1$	$5+5$
$3+1=$	$3+3$	$7+1$	$5+4$	$6+4$
$2+2=$	$4+2$	$4+4$	$6+3$	$8+2$
$4+1=$	$6+1$	$5+3$	$7+2$	$7+3$
$2-1=1$	$5-2$	$7-2$	$8-2$	$10-1$
$3-1=$	$6-1$	$7-3$	$9-1$	$10-5$
$4-1=$	$6-3$	$8-1$	$9-4$	$10-4$
$4-2=$	$6-2$	$8-4$	$9-3$	$10-2$
$5-1=$	$7-1$	$8-3$	$9-2$	$10-3$

10. Written Exercises in Subtraction.

For the first practice in written subtraction, Chart II. may be used. The children must learn the meaning of the sign of subtraction (—, less) and use this in representing the results of their observation. By observing all the dots in the rectangles, and then covering first those in the right and then those in the left, the following results will be reached:

A. $2-1=1$, $4-2=2$, B. $2-1=1$, $4-2=2$,
$3-1=2$, $5-1=4$, $3-2=1$, $5-4=1$,
$4-1=3$, $5-2=3$, $4-3=1$, $5-3=2$,
etc. etc. etc. etc.

When Chart II. can be observed, and the corresponding figures readily written, the process should be reversed. The children should produce the numbers when the figures are shown. The work on the pupils' slates may assume this form.

$5 - 2 = 3.$

The lower part of Chart IV. furnishes a convenient means of drill in the interpretation of figures denoting subtraction.

As a final review of this kind of work, Chart V. will be useful, inasmuch as it requires the pupil to interpret the signs $+$ and $-$, as well as to indicate operations.

CHART V.

For Review of Chart II.

$7+1$	$8-5$	$3-1$	$2-1$	$5-3$	$7-2$	$10-9$
$2+1$	$2+6$	$5-1$	$9-8$	$6+1$	$4-1$	$10-3$
$4+4$	$8-2$	$6-5$	$4+5$	$2+8$	$5+3$	$10-7$
$8+1$	$9-4$	$8-1$	$6+3$	$1+1$	$8+2$	$3+7$
$8-4$	$2+2$	$1+7$	$3-2$	$6-1$	$4+6$	$10-8$
$1+5$	$2+5$	$6-4$	$9-5$	$7-1$	$5-2$	$10-2$
$8-3$	$3+1$	$1+4$	$6-2$	$1+6$	$3+3$	$10-6$
$5+2$	$9-7$	$5+4$	$9+1$	$2+4$	$2+7$	$2+3$
$5-4$	$1+2$	$5+1$	$5+5$	$3+2$	$7-5$	$10-4$
$4+1$	$6+2$	$3+4$	$3+5$	$7+3$	$4+2$	$6+4$
$8-7$	$8-6$	$7-4$	$1+3$	$3+6$	$1+9$	$10-5$
$1+8$	$4+3$	$7-3$	$7-6$	$7+2$	$6-3$	$9-6$

11. COMBINED ADDITION AND SUBTRACTION.

Up to this point the written exercises have been connected immediately with the observation of the chart. Nothing more has been required of the children than the translating of the number pictures into figures, and figures into number pictures. Now, in order to free the written work from the necessity of observation; to replace immediate knowledge of objects with ideas of objects, the results of the additions and subtractions may be united in the same written exercises, so that the one may furnish the clew to the other, thus:

$$2 + 1 = 3. \qquad 3 - 1 = 2.$$
$$1 + 2 = 3. \qquad 3 - 2 = 1.$$

The whole of Chart V. may be treated in this way.

While exercises in multiplication and division have not been hitherto excluded, they are not numerous enough in this stage to make it worth while to introduce them into the written work as special topics.

Before proceeding to explain the treatment of numbers in the following stage of the work, I will remark that it is of the utmost importance that the work in numbers from one to ten should be thoroughly mastered. Naming any number up to, and including, ten, and also one part of the number, should instantly suggest to the child the other part. The two parts of each number should be so associated with each other and with the number that one part cannot be thought of as such without the idea of the other part being at once called to mind. Haste here is not to be desired. The results must be lastingly fixed, and this can only be accomplished by much patient, attentive, earnest effort.

I have suggested a progressive use of a few kinds of apparatus, but I would by no means limit the teacher to these. Variety of illustration is desirable; but it is also desirable to have some means of making the children do such work as will cause the desired results, which will not be a constant drain upon the teacher's power. Hence the free use of the charts for review is recommended.

CHAPTER II.

NUMBERS FROM ONE TO TWENTY.

12. COUNTING TO TWENTY.

As in teaching numbers from one to ten we began with counting, so we do in teaching numbers from ten to twenty. Put ten balls on the upper wire of the numeral frame. Let the children find how many *twos* there are in ten, how many *fives*, how many *tens*, and how many *ones*. Then tell them that ten ones are called a ten, and that one is called a unit. Count out ten units on the upper wire, and call the result one ten. Put one ball out on the second wire; then, pointing first to the ten and next to the one, say: "One ten and one unit make eleven units." Add another ball, and then, pointing as before, say: "One ten and two units are twelve units." And so proceed to the sentence: "One ten and nine units make nineteen units."

Add another ball, and there appear two rows of ten each, thus:

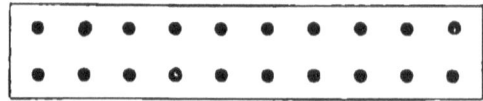

The truth which the pupils gain from observing

these balls is expressed: Two rows are two tens, or twenty units. These dots should then be copied by the children on their slates from a copy made on the board by the teacher.

For further practice let the above sentences be repeated as the balls are shown, from ten to twenty; and then let the counting from one to twenty be practised, introducing the following changes:

1. One, two, three, four, five, and so on to twenty.
2. After one comes two, after two comes three, and so on to twenty.
3. One and one are two, two and one are three, and so on.
4. One, three, five, seven, etc.
5. Two, four, six, eight, etc.
6. One, four, seven, ten, etc.
7. Two, five, eight, eleven, etc.
8. Three, six, nine, twelve, etc.
9. Twenty, nineteen, eighteen, etc.
10. Before twenty comes nineteen, etc.
11. Twenty less one is nineteen, etc.
12. Twenty, eighteen, sixteen, etc.
13. Nineteen, seventeen, fifteen, etc.
14. Twenty, seventeen, fourteen, etc.

When the children can surely and readily perform these exercises; can unite a ten and a fundamental number — that is, a number from one to ten; can change any number from eleven to twenty into tens and units; and when they can, further, construct any number on their slates by arranging the proper dots in tens and units; and can name any number shown them by balls or marks,—then and not till then, may they be allowed to pass on to the representation in figures of numbers from eleven to twenty. Till they have reached this ability, they may be kept practising upon the written work connected with numbers from one to ten. This will constitute a valuable review.

Written work should never precede corresponding oral work; for the written work, at this stage, is simply designed to impress upon the mind what the oral work has already made clear to the understanding. It is useful for review, but should keep a few steps behind the oral work, whenever the children are introduced to a new topic. Written work demands more self-independence; but in classes composed of several divisions the pupils must be thrown more upon their own resources. On account of the weaker children, therefore, the written exercises should be deferred till a perfect understanding is gained and a certain degree of facility is reached. It is well to bear this remark in mind constantly.

The written representation of numbers from eleven to twenty is not difficult for children to comprehend. The figure standing for the ten is put at the left, that representing the units at the right, therefore:

$$1 \text{ ten and } 1 \text{ unit} = 11 \text{ units.}$$
$$1 \text{ ten and } 2 \text{ units} = 12 \text{ units.}$$

1 ten and 3 units = 13 units, and so on to nineteen. The following series may be explained and copied:

10 + 1 = 11.	10 + 8 = 18.	14 + 1 = 15.
10 + 2 = 12.	10 + 9 = 19.	15 + 1 = 16.
10 + 3 = 13.	10 + 10 = 20.	16 + 1 = 17.
10 + 4 = 14.	10 + 1 = 11.	17 + 1 = 18.
10 + 5 = 15.	11 + 1 = 12.	18 + 1 = 19.
10 + 6 = 16.	12 + 1 = 13.	19 + 1 = 20.
10 + 7 = 17.	13 + 1 = 14.	

13. Separating Numbers into Two Parts.

In general the same course is to be followed in the division, or separation, of numbers from eleven to

CHART VI.
Uniting and Separating Numbers from Eleven to Twenty.

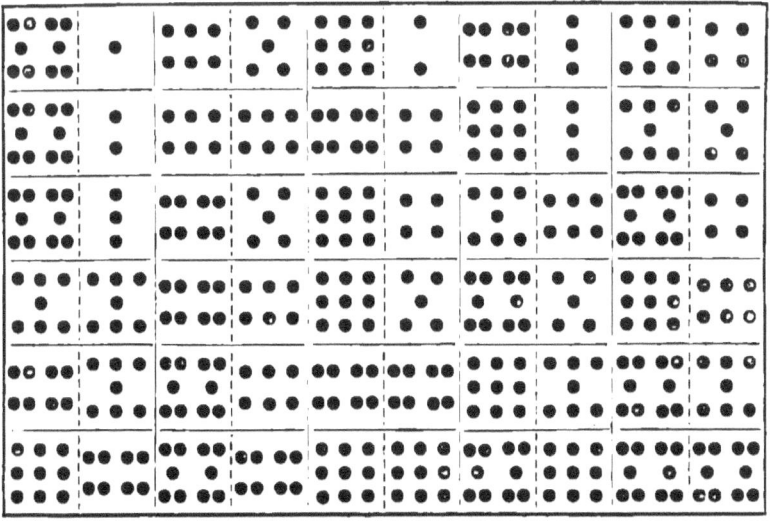

twenty as was recommended in regard to numbers from one to ten. The results needed in all the fundamental rules may be obtained by observing the separation of the several numbers into the various pairs of which they are composed, as shown on the preceding chart.

The treatment of numbers at this stage of the work is almost the same, in general, as in the case of numbers below ten. The division of each number between eleven and twenty is to be indicated by the arrangement of the balls on the numeral frame by the teacher. From each division two results in addition and two in subtraction are to be obtained; and, in the case of numbers composed of factors, at least one result for division and one for multiplication. No division is to be made, however, that will make one part of the divided number greater than ten. The division of the numbers here meant is simply the separation of the numbers into two parts.

The divisions are to be carefully shown, one after another, the number-pictures made by the children, and the truth stated orally, with frequent repetition, before the chart is called into use. The chart is for review only: first, by reciting the facts as shown by the arrangement of dots; second, by copying the number-pictures on the slates; and, third, by representing the dots by figures.

I will first indicate the results to be reached, and then make suggestions as to the manner of doing the work.

SEPARATING NUMBERS INTO TWO PARTS. 49

THE NUMBER ELEVEN.

Eleven can be divided into:

a. Ten and one; hence,
$$10 + 1 = 11, \qquad 11 - 1 = 10,$$
$$1 + 10 = 11, \qquad 11 - 10 = 1.$$

b. Six and five; hence,
$$6 + 5 = 11, \qquad 11 - 5 = 6,$$
$$5 + 6 = 11, \qquad 11 - 6 = 5.$$

c. Nine and two; hence,
$$9 + 2 = 11, \qquad 11 - 2 = 9,$$
$$2 + 9 = 11, \qquad 11 - 9 = 2.$$

d. Eight and three; hence,
$$8 + 3 = 11, \qquad 11 - 3 = 8,$$
$$3 + 8 = 11, \qquad 11 - 8 = 3.$$

e. Seven and four; hence,
$$7 + 4 = 11, \qquad 11 - 4 = 7,$$
$$4 + 7 = 11, \qquad 11 - 7 = 4.$$

THE NUMBER TWELVE.

Twelve can be divided into:

a. Ten and two;
$$10 + 2 = 12, \qquad 12 - 2 = 10,$$
$$2 + 10 = 12, \qquad 12 - 10 = 2.$$

b. Six and six;
$$6 + 6 = 12, \qquad \text{6 in 12 two times,}$$
$$12 - 6 = 6, \qquad 6 \times 2 = 12,$$
$$2 \times 6 = 12, \qquad \tfrac{1}{6} \text{ of } 12 = 2,$$
$$\tfrac{1}{2} \text{ of } 12 = 6, \qquad \text{2 in 12 six times.}$$

c. Eight and four;

$8 + 4 = 12,$ $12 - 8 = 4,$
$4 + 8 = 12,$ $3 \times 4 = 12,$
$12 - 4 = 8,$ $\tfrac{1}{3}$ of $12 = 4,$

4 in 12 three times.

d. Nine and three;

$9 + 3 = 12,$ $12 - 9 = 3,$
$3 + 9 = 12,$ $4 \times 3 = 12,$
$12 - 3 = 9,$ $\tfrac{1}{4}$ of $12 = 3,$

3 in 12 four times.

e. Seven and five;

$7 + 5 = 12,$ $12 - 5 = 7,$
$5 + 7 = 12,$ $12 - 7 = 5.$

THE NUMBER THIRTEEN.

Thirteen can be divided into:

a. Ten and three;

$10 + 3 = 13,$ $13 - 3 = 10,$
$3 + 10 = 13,$ $13 - 10 = 3.$

b. Eight and five;

$8 + 5 = 13,$ $13 - 5 = 8,$
$5 + 8 = 13,$ $13 - 8 = 5.$

c. Nine and four;

$9 + 4 = 13,$ $13 - 4 = 9,$
$4 + 9 = 13,$ $13 - 9 = 4.$

d. Seven and six;

$7 + 6 = 13,$ $13 - 6 = 7,$
$6 + 7 = 13,$ $13 - 7 = 6.$

SEPARATING NUMBERS INTO TWO PARTS. 51

THE NUMBER FOURTEEN.

Fourteen can be divided into:

a. Ten and four;

$10+4$, $\quad 4+10$, $\quad 14-4$, $\quad 14-10$.

b. Seven and seven;

$7+7$, $\quad 14-7$, $\quad 2\times 7$, $\quad 7$ in 14, $\frac{1}{2}$ of 14.

c. Eight and six;

$8+6$, $\qquad 14-8$, $\qquad \frac{1}{7}$ of 14,
$6+8$, $\qquad 7\times 2$, $\qquad 2$ in 14.
$14-6$,

d. Nine and five;

$9+5$, $\quad 5+9$, $\quad 14-5$, $\quad 14-9$.

THE NUMBER FIFTEEN.

Fifteen can be divided into:

a. Ten and five;

$10+5$, $\qquad 15-10$, $\qquad \frac{1}{3}$ of 15,
$5+10$, $\qquad 3\times 5$, $\qquad 5$ in 15.
$15-5$,

b. Nine and six;

$9+6$, $\qquad 15-9$, $\qquad \frac{1}{5}$ of 15,
$6+9$, $\qquad 5\times 3$, $\qquad 3$ in 15.
$15-6$,

c. Eight and seven;

$8+7$, $\quad 7+8$, $\quad 15-7$, $\quad 15-8$.

THE NUMBER SIXTEEN.

Sixteen can be divided into:

a. Ten and six;
  $10 + 6,$ $6 + 10,$ $16 - 6,$ $16 - 10.$

b. Eight and eight;
  $8 + 8,$ $8 \times 2,$ $4 \times 4,$ 4 in 16.
  $16 - 8,$ $\frac{1}{2}$ of 16,   2 in 16,
  $2 \times 8,$ $\frac{1}{8}$ of 16, $\frac{1}{4}$ of 16,

c. Nine and seven;
  $9 + 7,$ $7 + 9,$ $16 - 7,$ $16 - 9.$

THE NUMBER SEVENTEEN.

Seventeen can be divided into:

a. Ten and seven;
  $10 + 7,$ $7 + 10,$ $17 - 7,$ $17 - 10.$

b. Nine and eight;
  $9 + 8,$ $8 + 9,$ $17 - 8,$ $17 - 9.$

THE NUMBER EIGHTEEN.

Eighteen can be divided into:

a. Ten and eight;
  $10 + 8,$ $18 - 10,$ $9 \times 2,$ 9 in 18,
  $8 + 10,$ $18 - 8,$ $\frac{1}{9}$ of 18,   2 in 18.

b. Nine and nine;
  $9 + 9,$ 9 in 18, $6 \times 3,$
  $18 - 9,$ $3 \times 6,$ $\frac{1}{6}$ of 18,
  $2 \times 9,$ $\frac{1}{3}$ of 18,   6 in 18.
  $\frac{1}{2}$ of 18,   6 in 18,

THE NUMBER NINETEEN.

Nineteen can be divided into:

Ten and nine;

$10 + 9,$ $\quad 9 + 10,$ $\quad 19 - 9,$ $\quad 19 - 10.$

THE NUMBER TWENTY.

Twenty can be divided into:

Ten and ten;

$10 + 10,$	10 in 20,	$5 \times 4,$
$20 - 10,$	$4 \times 5,$	$\frac{1}{5}$ of 20,
$2 \times 10,$	$\frac{1}{4}$ of 20,	4 in 20.
$\frac{1}{2}$ of 20,	5 in 20,	

14. TEACHING NUMBERS FROM ELEVEN TO TWENTY.

It has already been remarked that it is of the highest importance for the pupils to know every two parts of which each number from one to ten consists. As an indication of the way the work in developing a knowledge of numbers from eleven to twenty should be managed, I will show by a few examples how to utilize this knowledge of the parts of the fundamental numbers.

If 5 is to be added to 8, let 2 be added first, so as to make 10. If this 2 be taken from the 5, 3 remains; and this 3 added to 10 makes thirteen; therefore, 5 added to 8 makes 13. In general, first add enough to make 10; then add the rest of the number to be added.

If 5 is to be subtracted from 13, first subtract 3, so that the remainder will be 10; then from the 10 take away the rest of the 5, namely, 2, and the remainder is 8.

The relations, or truths, shown by the number pictures for 8 and 5, may be indicated as follows:

$8 + 5$ may be resolved into $8 + 2 = 10$; $10 + 3 = 13$.
$5 + 8$ may be resolved into $5 + 5 = 10$; $10 + 3 = 13$.
$13 - 5$ may be resolved into $13 - 3 = 10$; $10 - 2 = 8$.
$13 - 8$ may be resolved into $13 - 3 = 10$. $10 - 5 = 5$.

The numbers 9 and 7 may be treated thus:

$9 + 7$ may be changed into $9 + 1 = 10$; $10 + 6 = 16$.
$7 + 9$ may be changed into $7 + 3 = 10$; $10 + 6 = 16$.
$16 - 7$ may be changed into $16 - 6 = 10$; $10 - 1 = 9$.
$16 - 9$ may be changed into $16 - 6 = 10$; $10 - 3 = 7$.

These processes and results are first to be shown by means of the balls on the numeral frame, then by the number pictures, which are first to be made by the teacher on the board and afterwards copied by the children on the slates. As fast as the number pictures have been treated in this way, Chart VI. may be used as a means of review.

The chart is to be read from left to right, right to left, top to bottom, and bottom to top. If the child hesitates in this reading, the teacher should lead him to see the divisions of the numbers to be added or subtracted, such that the results first obtained will always be 10. By this means the pupil will learn to think to the desired result without counting. When this reading of the chart can be gone through with rapidly and correctly, the chart may be copied picture by picture, thus :

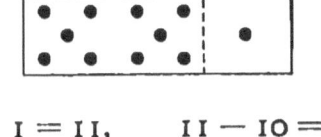

10 + 1 = 11,   11 − 10 = 1,
1 + 10 = 11,   11 − 1 = 10.

Next should follow the reverse of this process, namely, writing the corresponding number pictures when the figures are given. On Chart VII. are the figures corresponding to the number pictures on Chart VI. Let the pupils copy these figures, and at first produce the corresponding pictures ; but later the results may be written immediately in figures, or recited orally.

CHART VII.

WRITTEN REPRESENTATION OF CHART VI.

10 + 1	6 + 6	9 + 4	10 + 5	10 + 7
6 + 5	8 + 4	7 + 6	9 + 6	9 + 8
9 + 2	9 + 3	10 + 4	8 + 7	10 + 8
8 + 3	7 + 5	7 + 7	10 + 6	9 + 9
7 + 4	10 + 3	8 + 6	8 + 8	10 + 9
10 + 2	8 + 5	9 + 5	9 + 7	10 + 10
11 − 1	12 − 6	13 − 4	15 − 5	17 − 7
11 − 5	12 − 4	13 − 6	15 − 6	17 − 8
11 − 2	12 − 3	14 − 4	15 − 7	18 − 8
11 − 3	12 − 5	14 − 7	16 − 6	18 − 9
11 − 4	13 − 3	14 − 6	16 − 8	19 − 9
12 − 2	13 − 5	14 − 5	16 − 7	20 − 10

Charts VIII. and IX. are designed to assist in the final review of the addition and subtraction of numbers from one to twenty. This work completes the learning of the tables of addition and subtraction, which was begun in sections 9 and 10, and hence should be made very thorough. These charts should be copied by the children. Sometimes the corresponding pictures should be constructed, and sometimes the results should be written at once in figures. The drill should be partly oral; at one time the pupil reading from the chart and giving the result; at another, the teacher should read. The work may be varied by letting the reading and reciting both be done by pupils.

CHART VIII.

FOR REVIEW OF CHART VI.

16 − 6	9 + 5	12 − 7	9 + 6	3 + 10
10 + 1	15 − 5	10 + 3	9 + 8	2 + 10
8 + 4	11 − 4	6 + 5	18 − 8	17 − 10
13 − 3	12 − 6	12 − 4	19 − 9	14 − 10
12 − 5	14 − 8	11 − 1	7 + 5	16 − 10
9 + 2	8 − 8	4 + 7	12 − 9	7 + 10
13 − 8	10 + 6	9 + 4	10 + 2	1 + 10
5 + 7	17 − 7	13 − 9	12 − 8	8 + 10
13 − 5	9 + 3	11 − 2	6 + 6	19 − 10
3 + 8	11 − 3	8 + 6	8 + 5	6 + 10

CHART IX.

FOR REVIEW OF CHART VI.

4 + 9	12 − 3	11 − 9	14 − 4	18 − 10
11 − 5	7 + 4	14 − 6	7 + 7	11 − 10
12 − 2	4 + 8	10 + 9	2 + 9	4 + 10
5 + 9	5 + 8	15 − 9	14 − 9	15 − 10
15 − 6	13 − 7	16 − 8	6 + 8	10 + 10
11 − 8	5 + 6	3 + 9	6 + 9	5 + 10
11 − 7	10 + 4	11 − 6	10 + 7	20 − 10
10 + 5	6 + 7	13 − 6	17 − 9	12 − 10
18 − 9	14 − 7	8 + 3	10 + 8	9 + 10
9 + 9	14 − 5	7 + 6	17 − 8	13 − 10

If you exercise the children upon numbers from ten to twenty, as was recommended in regard to numbers from one to ten, namely, by having the results of the additions and subtractions reached in all cases through the performing of the necessary operations upon the objects themselves, and then by having the results fixed in the memory through the repetition of the processes by which they were reached, and not by the saying of the sentences which express the results, you will have laid a most thorough foundation for the following stage; that is, the treatment of numbers from twenty to one hundred. But not every child possesses a sufficiently strong memory for numbers. It would be tiresome to dwell on this stage of the work till every child was perfect in all the operations practised. This perfection is to be reached in the next stage of the work, where the exercises are similar, where they are more varied, and where, on account of their greater variety, they are less fatiguing.

It always makes a difference whether a child is taught alone, or with many others, as in school. In the one case, the work may be graduated to the individual; but in school, if one attempts to make the weakest perfect, the brightest, and even those of moderate talent, are kept back too much. In school, neither the brightest nor the dullest, but the average, must determine the progress of the class. All must always be made to comprehend the work in hand, at least so far as is necessary for understanding what is to follow; but readiness in doing may often be secured through the reviews necessarily practised in what follows. In this case addition and subtraction of numbers above twenty will make imperfections here disappear, if the same processes are continued.

Special attention ought to be given to the numbers 12, 15, 16, 18, and 20, because they afford an opportunity to prepare the children for multiplication and division. The following suggestions are offered:

$\frac{1}{2}$ year = 6 months; $\frac{2}{2}$ year = 12 months.
$\frac{1}{3}$ " = 4 " ; $\frac{2}{3}$ " = 8 "
$\frac{1}{4}$ " = 3 " ; $\frac{2}{4}$ " = 6 "
$\frac{1}{6}$ " = 2 " ; $\frac{2}{6}$ " = 4 "
$\frac{1}{12}$ " = 1 " ; $\frac{2}{12}$ " = ·2 "

If 1 apple costs 2 cents, what cost 2, 3, 4, 5, 6 apples?

1	"	3	"	"	2, 3, 4 apples?
1	"	4	"	"	2, 3 apples?
6	"	12	"	"	1, 2, 3, 4, 5 apples?
4	"	12	"	"	1, 2, 3 apples?
3	"	12	"	"	1, 2 apples?
2	"	12	"	"	1 apple?

The written work on numbers from ten to twenty is to follow the illustrations of Chart VI., as previously indicated.

It is recommended that the addition and subtraction should be limited to the fundamental numbers, because additions in the second ten are grounded upon those in the first ten.

If the child knows that:

    $1 + 3 = 4$, he knows that $11 + 3 = 14$.
    $2 + 6 = 8$, " " $12 + 6 = 18$.
    $4 + 3 = 7$, " " $14 + 3 = 17$.

It is only necessary to call his attention to these facts.

CHAPTER III.

NUMBERS FROM ONE TO ONE HUNDRED.

15. COUNTING.

For the purpose of extending the ideas of numbers to one hundred use should be made of the large numeral frame with 100 balls. First move out two rows of balls on the frame. These, as the children already know, contain 2 tens, or 20 units.

Add to these another row, and we have now

so may be shown
3 tens, or 30 units;
4 tens, or 40 units,
5 tens, or 50 units,
6 tens, or 60 units,
7 tens, or 70 units,
8 tens, or 80 units,
9 tens, or 90 units,
10 tens, or 100 units.

The statements of the truths thus exhibited may be practised by

a. Naming the numbers in order, forwards and backwards;

b. Questioning on the numbers out of their order;

c. Pointing and having the children name;

d. Naming and having the children point;

e. Forming the series in order and having them named:

$$10 + 10 = 20; \ 20 + 10 = 30, \text{ etc.}$$
$$100 - 10 = 90; \ 90 - 10 = 80, \text{ etc.}$$

The expression of the numbers in figures should be omitted at first, so that the ideas of the numbers may not be confused with the figures. If written work for the pupils is desired, enough may be found in a review of the work on numbers from ten to twenty.

Now the teacher may go back again to one ten, and have the numbers 11, 12, 13, and so on to 20, formed by the addition of one unit at a time, as was recommended in the development of numbers from ten to twenty. In the same way should the numbers from 21 to 30, 31 to 40, 41 to 50, etc., to 100 be formed. The numerical facts thus illustrated may be expressed:

Twenty and one are twenty-one;
Twenty and two are twenty-two;
Twenty and three are twenty-three;
and so on to 100; and also,
Two tens and one unit are twenty-one units;
Two tens and two units are twenty-two units;
Two tens and three units are twenty-three units,
and so on to 100.

At each new ten the teacher should stop and practise the children in the numbers already learned, by questioning them on the numbers out of their order. For example, point to 24, 27, 29, 22, or 30 balls, and ask, How many balls? Tell the pupil to point to different numbers. Pointing to 25, ask, How many tens and how many units are there? What is the number called? How many is it more than 20? How many less than 30? Ask:

What number comes after 25, 22, 29?
What number comes before 25, 22, 29?
Count forward from 1 to 30.
Count backward from 30 to 1.
Count 2, 4, 6, 8, 10, and so on to 30.
Count 1, 3, 5, 7, 9, and so on to 29.
Count 30, 28, 26, 24, and so on to 0.
Count 29, 27, 25, 23, and so on to 1.

With the introduction of each ten review from the beginning.

When the school is not furnished with a large numeral frame, a chart like the following, Chart X., may be used as a means of giving the children an intuitive knowledge of numbers from one to one hundred, and of the decimal system of numbers. Both the top and bottom parts of the chart may be used for counting by tens. If a piece of stiff pasteboard or a ruler be cut in this form, it may be so

held as to cover any number of units in any row; and so by moving it down the lower part of the chart, and then across the chart, the formation of all numbers from one to one hundred may be shown to the eye, the same as by the numeral frame.

CHART X.

COUNTING BY TENS.

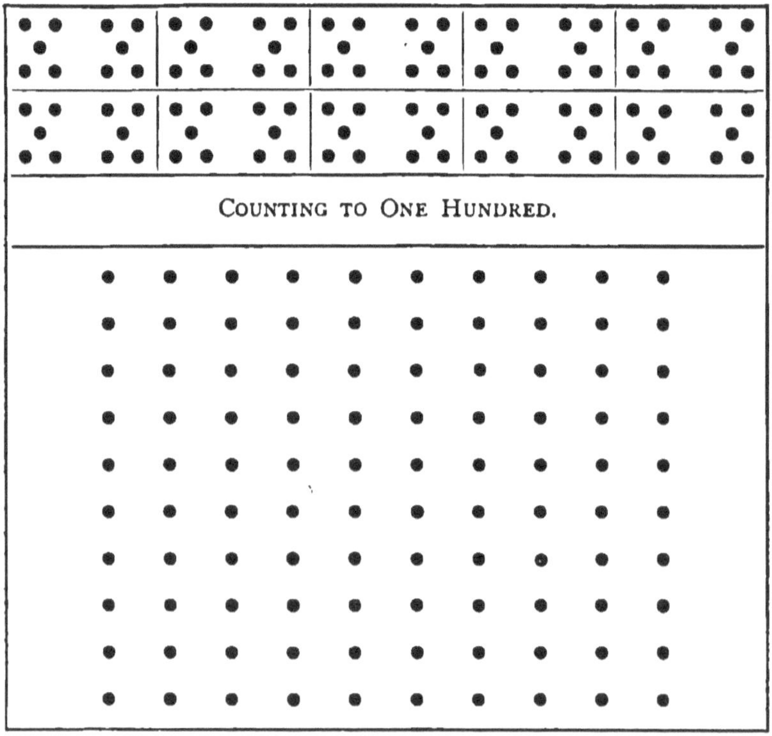

COUNTING TO ONE HUNDRED.

Chart X. may be used profitably as a means of reviewing numbers from one to one hundred, either by counting by tens or counting by units; or for

READING AND WRITING NUMBERS. 65

showing numbers to be named, or to be reduced to tens and units; or for showing any number of tens and units that may be named; as well as for various other exercises.

16. READING AND WRITING NUMBERS.

Written work, that is, use of figures, should not be introduced till the pupils are able to find any number on the numeral frame or on the chart, to resolve any number which may be shown on the chart or frame into tens and units, or to unite any number of tens and units into the number which they constitute. It

CHART XI.

WRITTEN REPRESENTATION OF CHART X.

1	2	3	4	5	6	7	8	9	10
11	12	13	14	15	16	17	18	19	20
21	22	23	24	25	26	27	28	29	30
31	32	33	34	35	36	37	38	39	40
41	42	43	44	45	46	47	48	49	50
51	52	53	54	55	56	57	58	59	60
61	62	63	64	65	66	67	68	69	70
71	72	73	74	75	76	77	78	79	80
81	82	83	84	85	86	87	88	89	90
91	92	93	94	95	96	97	98	99	100

is of the utmost importance at this stage of the work that figures are not mistaken for numbers; and to secure this, much work should be done with objects that can be numbered, before the pupils are introduced to the use of figures, which are the mere signs of the numbers themselves.

The preceding chart, Chart XI., corresponds to Chart X. It is simply the written signs of the numbers which the children have just learned.

A word as to the use of this chart. The children are to read the expressions of the different numbers in figures, to find the expression for any number which the teacher may name, to find the expression of any number which the teacher may show on Chart X., and to show upon Chart X. the number corresponding to any figures to which the teacher may point.

If the children understand into how many tens and units any number may be separated, it will generally be sufficient to tell them that the tens are written at the left and the units at the right. Chart XI. may now be copied by the pupils. The teacher may now have the expressions for different numbers which he finds on the chart read and then copied.

To impress the written expressions of the different numbers from one to one hundred upon the minds of the pupils, the following series may be constructed and written by the children:

$$1+1=2; \quad 2+1=3; \quad 3+1=4,$$

and so on to 100.

17. ADDITION.

In the two first courses, that is, in the study of numbers from one to ten, and of numbers from one to twenty, we have recommended the simultaneous treatment of the four ground rules of addition, subtraction, multiplication, and division. At this point they should be separated. A few words in explanation of the reason will be added.

With the size of numbers the parts into which the numbers can be separated multiply; so that the point is soon reached where the resulting facts can no longer be impressed upon the memory, and, indeed, where this is no longer necessary. As a rule, the memory is to be burdened with those facts only which constitute the foundation upon which future progress depends; for example, the addition and subtraction tables. In teaching these we were able to ground all the written exercises upon the direct observation of the charts and other objects; but in the treatment of higher numbers this is impossible. But the ability of the pupils at this point has so increased that they are able to solve a much larger number of problems in the same time. We must be able, therefore, especially where there are several divisions to be occupied at the same time, to select problems which will be easy to assign, which will make the work of correction easy, and which will afford much occupation for the pupils.

More than this, arithmetic is partly an art, and in art facility in doing presupposes practice. Facility, however, can never be attained unless the same thing is practised for a long time. If a piano player wishes to make a movement absolutely his own, it is not enough for him to practise it in its turn along with twenty other movements; he must repeat this movement by itself over and over. So facility in a definite numerical operation, be it addition or subtraction or any other, is attained only through continued practice in this very operation. This practice, however, must not be mere mechanical routine, but rather, thoughtful practice. To secure this, careful work must be done in the addition of units.

The instruction must begin with what is easiest, and proceed gradually to the most difficult; begin with the addition of two, then add three, and so on to nine. The exercises are to be given at first with the help of apparatus for actual observation; but gradually the apparatus is to be dispensed with, and the pupils are to be taught to reach the required results by processes of thinking. The following may serve as an example of the proper work in teaching the addition of units to tens or to tens and units. Suppose the number seven is to be added to one and to the succeeding results; the steps would be as follows:

$1 + 7 = 8$, which is already known.
$8 + 7 = 15$, may be thought as $8 + 2 = 10$, and $10 + 5 = 15$.

ADDITION.

$15 + 7 = 22$, may be thought as $15 + 5 = 20$, and $20 + 2 = 22$.
$22 + 7 = 29$, may be thought as $2 + 7 = 9$, and $20 + 9 = 29$.
$29 + 7 = 36$, may be thought as $29 + 1 = 30$, and $30 + 6 = 36$.
$36 + 7 = 43$, may be thought as $36 + 4 = 40$, and $40 + 3 = 43$.
$43 + 7 = 50$, may be thought as $3 + 7 = 10$, and $40 + 10 = 50$.

$50 + 7 = 57$.

$57 + 7 = 64$, may be thought as $57 + 3 = 60$, and $60 + 4 = 64$.
$64 + 7 = 71$, may be thought as $64 + 6 = 70$, and $70 + 1 = 71$.
$71 + 7 = 78$, may be thought as $7 + 1 = 8$, and $70 + 8 = 78$.
$78 + 7 = 85$, may be thought as $78 + 2 = 80$, and $80 + 5 = 85$.
$85 + 7 = 92$, may be thought as $85 + 5 = 90$, and $90 + 2 = 92$.
$92 + 7 = 99$, may be thought as $2 + 7 = 9$, and $90 + 9 = 99$.

If the result falls within the given ten, only the units are to be increased; but if the result reaches into the next ten, the given units are first to be increased to ten and the remaining units added to the next ten. Along with this exercise in the successive additions of seven, let the corresponding parts of the addition table be carefully practised. Write upon the board the numbers 1, 2, 5, 8, 3, 9, 7, 4, 6, and 10, and have the number 7 added to each, until the results are perfectly committed to memory. The separating of the number to be added into two parts, the adding of the first part to the units, and the adding of the second part to the next ten will disappear with continued practice; the addition of 26 and 7, for example, will soon be reduced to a single operation, when the pupil is perfectly familiar with the fact that $6 + 7 = 13$.

Facility in addition grounded upon a thorough memorizing of the addition table is the end for which the teacher should strive; but he will not succeed in having all pupils reach this facility in the time which can properly be given to the first steps in addition. If the teacher insists upon a perfect memorizing of the addition table by the weakest pupils, under all circumstances, before proceeding to the addition of larger numbers, he does a wrong to the brightest, because he holds them back upon the first stage of addition so long that they become weary of the work. This is a pedagogical sin, which avenges itself no less upon the individuals than upon the class. The reason for the unequal acquisition of facility lies in the unequal talent of the pupils for impressing numbers upon the memory. Number memory is not the same in all pupils.

The teacher may, however, console himself with

the reflection that clear understanding and definite comprehension of the process is of more use to the student than great facility in performing the process. Every exercise must be brought within the comprehension of the pupil before he is allowed to enter upon a new stage of work. The attainment of a reasonable amount of facility is no less desirable in arithmetic than in other branches of study; and yet arithmetic has this advantage, that the following stages always take up the exercises of the preceding, and thus furnish an opportunity to increase the pupil's facility in preceding processes.

Even in private instruction it would not be advisable to keep a pupil of weak memory for numbers upon the first steps so long as would be required in order to reach the extreme of facility. To weary the pupil, to destroy his desire for arithmetical knowledge, is an injury which outweighs any facility in performing processes.

EXAMPLES.

One of the easiest ways of assigning examples for practice at this stage of the work is to have series of numbers formed, at first by the addition of the same number, later by the addition of different numbers alternately. Such series occupy profitably one division while the teacher is busy with another. A few written figures will indicate the desired lesson. A glance at the slate containing the pupil's work shows whether it is correct or not. The following examples will serve for explanation:

a.	b.	c.	d.
0+7= 7,	1+7= 8,	2+7= 9,	4+7= 11.
7+7=14,	8+7=15,	9+7=16,	11+7= 18.
14+7=21,	15+7=22,	16+7=23,	18+7= 25.
21+7=28,	22+7=29,	23+7=30,	25+7= 32.
28+7=35,	29+7=36,	30+7=37,	32+7= 39.
35+7=42,	36+7=43,	37+7=44,	39+7= 46.
42+7=49,	43+7=50,	44+7=51,	46+7= 53.
49+7=56,	50+7=57,	51+7=58,	53+7= 60.
56+7=63,	57+7=64,	58+7=65,	60+7= 67.
63+7=70,	64+7=71,	65+7=72,	67+7= 74.
70+7=77,	71+7=78,	72+7=79,	74+7= 81.
77+7=84,	78+7=85,	79+7=86,	81+7= 88.
84+7=91,	85+7=92,	86+7=93,	88+7= 95.
91+7=98,	92+7=99,	93+7=100,	95+7=102.

This table represents the pupil's work. The problems *a*, *b*, *c*, and *d* may be assigned by telling the class to add 7 to 0, 1, 2, and 4 fourteen times; or simply by writing 0 + 7, 1 + 7, etc.

Since the first numbers are 0, 1, 2, and 4, the results in any horizontal line vary by 1, 2, and 4, and so do the final results. A glance at one or two places in the vertical line and at the end will show whether the work is all right. The final results will be 14 × 7 plus 1, 2, and 4. So any series may be dictated, beginning with any number from 1 to 9, and adding any number from 1 to 9, and all the results known at a glance.

To give a greater variety, and at the same time provide for reviews, two numbers may be added alternately, for example:

$$2 + 4 = 6.$$
$$6 + 3 = 9.$$
$$9 + 4 = 13.$$
$$13 + 3 = 16.$$
$$16 + 4 = 20.$$
$$20 + 3 = 23, \text{ etc.}$$

Compare this with the series marked *c* above.

$$2 + 7 = 9.$$
$$9 + 7 = 16.$$
$$16 + 7 = 23, \text{ etc.}$$

and it is obvious that the series will end with 100.

A word in regard to written exercises in general. While it is true that in the beginning of the study of numbers figures are a positive hindrance, this is by no means universally the case. Written exercises are of the greatest importance, provided they are properly connected with observation and oral work. Practical life requires the use of written arithmetic and therefore the school must prepare the pupils for it. But the pedagogical reason is still stronger. Children are not all alike in ability. It often happens that in oral work the brightest pupils have too little to do in proportion to their ability, or that the weakest are behindhand in the solution of the problems, so that their real progress is hindered. Now written exercises, especially such series as have just been recommended, are adapted to all conditions of the class. Each can do in a given time what he is able, and all will do good work. The bright ones are not kept back, and the weakest are not overdriven. If all the work is not done by all the pupils, what is done is good for all. Written work, then, is adapted to all, while oral work is often adapted only to the average talent.

Moreover, exercises in written work for the class

CHART XII.

For Practice in the Ground Rules.

	a	b	c	d	e	f	g	h	i	k
l	1	12	26	34	47	53	67	76	84	96
m	2	19	22	31	43	52	70	73	87	93
n	5	16	28	39	41	55	63	77	83	94
o	8	17	21	33	44	59	62	75	86	97
p	3	15	27	36	49	51	68	72	90	92
q	7	20	24	32	46	58	61	80	82	99
r	4	13	29	38	42	54	66	71	88	95
s	9	18	23	40	45	57	64	79	85	91
t	6	11	30	35	50	56	65	74	89	98
u	10	14	25	37	48	60	69	78	81	100

allow the teacher time to give individual instruction to the weak pupils.

The preceding chart, marked Chart XII., will be found very useful in assigning work to be done outside the recitation hour, as well as for exercises, both oral and written, to be performed in the class. Let the numbers from one to ten be added to each of the numbers and we have one thousand examples in addition.

18. Subtraction.

Let the numbers 2, 3, 4, etc., to 10, be subtracted from 100 and from the successive remainders, and the exercises will be the reverse of those explained under addition; for example:

$100 - 7$ may be thought as $10 - 7 = 3$,
and $100 - 7 = 93$,
$93 - 7$ may be thought as $93 - 3 = 90$,
and $90 - 4 = 86$,
$86 - 7$ may be thought as $86 - 6 = 80$,
and $80 - 1 = 79$,
$79 - 7$ may be thought as $9 - 7 = 2$,
and $79 - 7 = 72$,
$72 - 7$ may be thought as $72 - 2 = 70$,
and $70 - 5 = 65$;

and so on till the remainder is less than seven.

If the minuend consists of tens only, the subtrahend is to be taken from 10, and the remainder added to the next ten below; for example: $100 - 7$

becomes $10-7=3$, and $90+3=93$. If the minuend consists of tens and units, and the units are more than the subtrahend, the subtrahend is to be taken from the units and the remainder added to the tens; for example: $79-7$ is changed to $9-7=2$ and $70+2=72$. If the minuend consists of tens and units, and the units are less than the subtrahend, the units of the minuend are to be subtracted first, and then from the tens are to be taken the difference between the units already subtracted and the subtrahend; for example: $93-7$ is changed to $93-3=90$, and $90-4=86$.

This shows us how important it was to teach the separation of the numbers below 10 into two parts; and also reminds us of the propriety of a careful review of the corresponding number before beginning a new exercise in subtraction. For example, before giving exercises in the subtracting of seven, the reviews should cover the following ground:

$$7=6+1 \text{ or } 1+6,$$
$$7=5+2 \text{ or } 2+5,$$
$$7=4+3 \text{ or } 3+4;$$

and also

$10-7$, $7-7$, $13-7$, $11-7$, $9-7$, $15-7$, $12-7$, $14-7$, $8-7$, $16-7$, and $17-7$.

In the addition of 9, the children will often reach the result by adding 10 and subtracting 1; so in subtracting 9, they will often reach the result by subtracting 10 and adding 1. Such practices should not be allowed unless they are understood; which will be the case if they are discovered by the children. But the teacher should examine and, if necessary, instruct.

It does not follow, however, that a pupil should be allowed to continue a practice in numerical computation simply because he has hit upon it and understands it. It is usually better for the teacher to train the pupils in the most expeditious methods of performing operations; and, as a rule, one method is better than two. For example, if the pupil is always required to reach results in the addition and subtraction of units in the way described above, whenever he is obliged to go through a conscious process in reaching the result, he will reach the point where such operations are automatic much quicker than he will if he is allowed to reach his results now by one process and now by another.

Written exercises may be given which are easy to correct, consisting of series of subtractions. The series, 100 − 7, etc., will end with 2; for 7 in 100 = 14, and 2 remainder. The series 99 − 8 ends with 3; since 99 ÷ 8 = 12, and 3 remainder. Thus exercises may be set consisting of a dozen or more subtractions, so constructed that a glance at the final result will show whether the work is correct.

Chart XII. may be made helpful in oral drill, since 1, 2, 3, etc., may be subtracted from each number; and thus the labor of the teacher may be materially lessened.

19. Connected Addition and Subtraction.

For the sake of variety, as well as for the purpose of reviewing the work of addition, series of alternate additions and subtractions may be given for written work; for example:

$$100 - 7 = 93,$$
$$93 + 4 = 97, \qquad 100 - 3 = 97;$$
$$97 - 7 = 90,$$
$$90 + 4 = 94, \qquad 97 - 3 = 94;$$
$$94 - 7 = 87,$$
$$87 + 4 = 91, \qquad 94 - 3 = 91;$$

and so on. Since subtracting 7 and adding 4 reduces a number 3, every second result must be the same as if 3 were subtracted.

$$1 + 7 = 8,$$
$$8 - 3 = 5, \qquad 1 + 4 = 5.$$
$$5 + 7 = 12,$$
$$12 - 3 = 9, \qquad 5 + 4 = 9, \text{ etc.}$$

Since adding 7 and subtracting 3 increases a number 4, every second result must be the same as if 4 were added.

Work of this kind is easy to assign and easy to examine. The above illustrations are designed merely as suggestions of what may be done.

So far in our treatment of numbers consisting of two places we have added and subtracted only units; but it would be a good preparation for work with

CONNECTED ADDITION AND SUBTRACTION. 79

numbers from 1 to 1,000 to add and subtract numbers larger than 10 at this stage. The following is suggested as a good order of work:

a. Tens to tens. *a.* Tens from tens
    $20 + 30$, $100 - 10$,
    $50 + 10$, $100 - 30$,
    $10 + 20$, etc. $90 - 70$, etc.

b. Tens to tens and units. *b.* Tens from tens and units.
    $36 + 40$, $96 - 40$,
    $30 + 40 = 70$; so $90 - 40 = 50$; so
    $36 + 40 = 76$. $96 - 40 = 56$.

c. Tens and units to tens. *c.* Tens and units from tens.
    $30 + 25$, $90 - 63$,
    $30 + 20 = 50$, $90 - 60 = 30$,
    $50 + 5 = 55$. $30 - 3 = 27$.

    d. Tens and units to tens and units.
        $32 + 44 = 32 + 40 + 4$,
        $68 + 28 = 68 + 20 + 8$.

    d. Tens and units from tens and units.
        $96 - 34 = 96 - 30 - 4$,
        $83 - 65 = 83 - 60 - 5$.

These exercises, at least those marked *a*, *b*, and *c*, should be readily performed by the pupils orally before they are changed to written exercises. In the written work, a union of addition and subtraction may take place in the same series of exercises, as shown below:

1. $10+20=30.$ 2. $10+30=40.$ 3. $100-30=70.$
   $30-10=20.$ $40-20=20.$ $70+20=90.$
   $20+20=40.$ $20+30=50.$ $90-30=60.$
   $40-10=30.$ $50-20=30.$ $60+20=80.$
   etc.   etc.   etc.

4. $100-20=$ 5. $10+40$ 6. $10+50$
   $+10$ -20 -30
7. $10+50$ 8. $100-40$ 9. $100-50$
   -40 $+20$ $+30$
10. $4+40$ 11. $7+50$ 12. $9+50$
    -20 -30 -40
13. $98-40$ 14. $96-50$ 15. $97-50$
    $+20$ $+30$ $+40$
16. $10+25$ 17. $10+46$ 18. $10+38$
    -20 -30 -20
19. $100-25$ 20. $100-46$ 21. $100-28$
    $+20$ $+30$ $+20$
22. $12+24$ 23. $7+36$ 24. $1+28$
    -12 -18 -14

Similar series of numbers may be given indefinitely as the needs of the class require.

The following rules may be useful:

To add one number between 10 and 100 to another, add first the tens and then the units; for example: $57+39$; $57+30=87$; $87+9=96$.

To subtract one number between 10 and 100 from another, subtract first the tens and then the units; for example: $77-49$; $77-40=37$; $37-9=28$.

A teacher ought to be satisfied with the weak

pupils if they can solve problems in these ways, and not try to teach them shorter processes. It is better for a pupil to be certain in one way than to be uncertain in several.

It was previously shown that there was great advantage in being able to increase any fundamental number to 10; there is a like advantage in being able to increase any number below a hundred to a hundred. It is well, therefore, to drill the pupils in such exercises as these:

86 and how many are 100?
$86 + 4 = 90$; $90 + 10 = 100$; hence 14.

67 and how many are 100?
$67 + 3 = 70$; $70 + 30 = 100$; hence 33.

48 and how many are 100?
$48 + 2 = 50$; $50 + 50 = 100$; hence 52.

Chart XII. affords abundant matter for drill in the addition of numbers below 100; for example, in adding 48 to each number on the chart, there are 100 additions. But each other number below 100 may be added; which makes 5,000 examples in addition. Or, by how many does 53 differ from each number on Chart XII.? In answering this, the child performs 100 subtractions. But the same may be asked of all the other numbers below 100; which gives 5,000 examples in subtraction. Add 24 to each number in the first five vertical columns; in the first four horizontal lines, etc. Remember that practice makes perfect.

20. Multiplication.

The multiplication table is the foundation of the process of multiplication. It is the tools without which neither multiplication nor division can be performed. Hence the child must make it so completely his own that it cannot be forgotten and that it will always be present to him in the twinkling of an eye when it is needed for use. It is in the power of the teacher to render such help to the little ones as will spare the tears which, without such help, will be sure to flow when the demand is made upon them to learn the multiplication table by heart.

If the teacher wishes happily to avoid these breakers he must be sure that two things always exist in proper relation one to the other, — intelligence and practice. Intelligence, which is gained only through direct observation, was formerly neglected; but the tendency at the present time is to neglect the practice. Instead of drilling the pupils thoroughly in the multiplication table in school, by means of recitations and questioning, and by means of connecting the work at every step with the preceding lessons, many teachers are satisfied with making the children understand how it is formed, and leaving the memorizing to be done as home lessons. But it is the special task of the teacher to show the children how they should learn. In order to point out to inexperienced teachers what exercises they may introduce to advantage while the pupils are committing the multiplication table to memory, it will be necessary to go somewhat into details.

Since thorough drill requires a long time, it is recommended to make a preparation for the learning of the multiplication table while teaching addition and subtraction. When the pupils have thoroughly learned to add and subtract the number two, they may be taught to multiply by two; when they have learned to add and subtract the number three, they may learn the threes of the multiplication table, etc. By this course sufficient time may be secured for reviews, which here are indispensably necessary, since upon them depends the impressing of numbers upon the memory.

21. Teaching the Multiplication Table.

TWOS OF THE MULTIPLICATION TABLE.

In our treatment of numbers from 1 to 20 we have already found once 2, 2 times 2, and so on to 10 times 2, and we will rejoice at whatever has remained in the memory; still it is necessary to develop the facts again.

Place two balls on the numeral frame, or two points on the board beside each other, thus:

• •

and ask, How many balls are there? Then put two more balls with them, thus:

• •

• •

and ask, How many times two balls are there? How many are two times two balls? How many are two times two? How many are two twos?

Just so may the ideas of 3, 4, 5, 6, 7, 8, 9, and 10 times 2 be developed. In doing this the following figure will be formed, and the following expressions of the truths which it represents should be repeated many times, both by individuals and in concert:

• •	Once	2	is	2.	10 times	2	are	20.
• •	2 times	2	are	4.	9 "	2	"	18.
• •	3 "	2	"	6.	8 "	2	"	16.
• •	4 "	2	"	8.	7 "	2	"	14.
• •	5 "	2	"	10.	6 "	2	"	12.
• •	6 "	2	"	12.	5 "	2	"	10.
• •	7 "	2	"	14.	4 "	2	"	8.
• •	8 "	2	"	16.	3 "	2	"	6.
• •	9 "	2	"	18.	2 "	2	"	4.
• •	10 "	2	"	20.	Once	2	is	2.

It will help if the children are led to find that, for example, 3 times 2 units are just as many units as 2 times 3 units. Thus, in the following figure there are 3 rows of 2 points each, and there are also 2 rows of 3 points each.

• •

• •

• •

So it may be shown that

4 times	2	are	8,	and 2 times	4	are	8.
5	"	2	"	10,	"	2	"	5	"	10.
6	"	2	"	12,	"	2	"	6	"	12.
7	"	2	"	14,	"	2	"	7	"	14.
8	"	2	"	16,	"	2	"	8	"	16.
9	"	2	"	18,	"	2	"	9	"	18.
10	"	2	"	20,	"	2	"	10	"	20.

The results stated at the right are already known as the sums of equal numbers. The one set of statements assists the pupil in remembering the other, yet the truths ought not to be confused. Practical examples like the following will guard against such confusion:

A mother gave her son 4 apples yesterday and 4 to-day; how many times did he receive 4 apples? How many are 2 times 4? How many times 4 is 8? How many fours can be made of 8?

A woman gives her child 2 apples daily; how many times 2 apples does he receive in 4 days? How many are 4 times 2? How many times 2 is 8? How many twos can be made of 8?

Let the children illustrate the multiplication table, as shown above, with points on their slates, and affix the results, thus:

• • 2,
• • 4,
• • 6, etc.

If they are to study the multiplication table at

home, let them first construct it; otherwise it is apt to have little meaning. The impressing of the facts out of their order is to be effected mainly through question and answer, and is proper work for the schoolroom. The more varied the practice, however, the more firmly the facts are impressed upon the memory. Hence the reverse form of viewing the facts is to be used. For example: How many times is 2 in 12? How many twos in 12? How often is 2 contained in 12? How often can we take 2 from 12? etc. It is well to spend a week or two on the number 2; and a portion of each lesson should be given to practical applications; for example:

1 whole	= 2 halves.	1 apple costs	2 cts.
2 wholes	= 4 halves.	2 apples cost	4 cts.
3 "	= 6 "	3 " "	6 "
etc.	etc.	etc.	etc.

THREES OF THE MULTIPLICATION TABLE.

• • • Let the course of instruction be as fol-
• • • lows:
• • •   *a.* Construct the table on the frame or
• • • board, as in the margin.
• • •   *b.* Practise alone and in concert forwards.
• • •   *c.* Practise alone and in concert back-
• • • wards.
• • •   *d.* Question out of the regular order.
• • •   *e.* Let the children make the same on
• • • their slates.

TEACHING THE MULTIPLICATION TABLE.

The results, 1, 2, 3, 4, 5, 6, and 10 times 3, the children will easily retain; for 3×2 has been already learned in studying the twos; 3×3, in studying the number picture for 9; 4×3, in the treatment of 12; 5×3, in the study of 15 on Chart VI.; 6×3, in the study of 18 on Chart VI.; and $10 \times 3 = 3 \times 10 = 3$ tens. These results will now afford little difficulty; 7, 8, and 9 times 3 will cause more. But $9 \times 3 = 10 \times 3 - 1 \times 3$; $7 \times 3 = 7+7+7$; $8 \times 3 = 8+8+8$; and all these are to be taught from rows of points.

The following applications are suggested:

> 1 orange costs 3 cents,
> 2 oranges cost 6 cents,
> 3 oranges cost 9 cents, etc.

FOURS OF THE MULTIPLICATION TABLE.

The course of exercises is the same as in teaching the twos and threes. More or less are already known of 1, 2, 3, 4, 5, and 10×4; so fix these numbers first. Connect 9×4 with 10×4; 6×4 with the known 5×4. Take special pains with 7×4 and 8×4. Apply as follows:

> 1 horse has 4 legs,
> 2 horses have 8 legs,
> 3 horses have 12 legs, etc.

FIVES OF THE MULTIPLICATION TABLE.

a. The pupil knows 1, 2, 3, 4, 5, 10×5.
b. He learns $5 \times 5 = 25$ easily from the sound.

c. $9 \times 5 = 10 \times 5 - 1 \times 5$.
d. $6 \times 5 = 5 \times 5$ and $5 = 30$.
e. $8 \times 5 = 2$ times $4 \times 5 = 2$ times 20, or 4 times $2 \times 5 = 4$ times 10.
f. 7×5 is to be connected with 6×5.

Always direct the practice so as to connect the thing to be learned with what precedes; first *a*, then *b*, then *a* and *b*; then *c*, then *a*, *b*, and *c*; then *d*, then *a*, *b*, *c*, *d*; then *e*, then *a*, *b*, *c*, *d*, *e*, etc. Apply thus: 1 five-cent piece = 6 cents, etc.

SIXES OF THE MULTIPLICATION TABLE.

a. 1, 2, 3, 4, 5, and 10×6 are known.
b. 6×6 is remembered by the sound.
c. 9×6 is to be connected with 10×6.
d. 7×6 is to be connected with 6×6.
e. 8×6 demands special work.

Application: 1 week has 6 working-days, etc.

SEVENS OF THE MULTIPLICATION TABLE.

a. 1, 2, 3, 4, 5, 6, and 10×7 are known.
b. 7×7 is easy to remember from the sound.
c. 9×7 is to be connected with 10×7.
d. 8×7 is to be connected with 7×7.

Application: 1 week has 7 days, etc.

EIGHTS OF THE MULTIPLICATION TABLE.

a. 1, 2, 3, 4, 5, 6, 7, 10×8 are known.
b. 8×8 is easy to learn from the sound.

c. $9 \times 8 = 10 \times 8 - 1 \times 8$.

Application: 8 boys sit in 1 row, etc.

NINES OF THE MULTIPLICATION TABLE.

a. 1, 2, 3, 4, 5, 6, 7, 8, 10 × 9 are known.

b. 9 × 9 is learned from the sound, also connected with 10 × 9.

Application: 1 yard costs 9 cents, etc.

TENS OF THE MULTIPLICATION TABLE.

The result is already known.

Application: 1 dime is worth 10 cents, etc.

If the children are made to observe, to recall, and to connect the unknown with the known, in the way just pointed out, they may soon be brought to understand any part of the multiplication table. But the teacher must discriminate sharply between understanding and knowing. Knowing presupposes continued practice and diligent repetition of what precedes; hence the pupil should never pass to a new sentence without reviewing what goes before. Let the new sentence be a reward for what is already learned, so that the children will be accustomed to find the reward for learning in the act of learning.

Knowing the multiplication table implies readiness for use. The child must remember only the result, not the process of reaching it. Question must follow answer instantly. In a word the multiplication table must be absolutely a thing of the memory. On thought of the words *seven times five* the thought of the word *thirty-five* must instantly follow. Perfect understanding comes through illustration; perfect memorizing, through diligent use and through frequent repetition almost endlessly continued.

What we have already explained is only a preparation for learning the multiplication table. This preparation was aimed at in the addition of numbers from one to a hundred; for example, when the pupil was exercised in the successive additions of six, ground was broken for learning the sixes of the table. The results can be fixed in the mind only through continuous application. All up to this point is only a preparation for learning the table in its written form.

22. Applying the Table to Written Work.

The written sign for multiplication is an inclined cross, thus, ×, and means time or times.

If we should write down the numbers from 1 to 10, and ask the pupils to use them successively as multipliers of a given number, we should by this means assist them to reach the results by the successive additions of the number to itself. However necessary this order may be in the development of the table and for its thorough comprehension, still a practical mastering of the same, a ready working knowledge of it, demands its application out of this order.

In order to fix in the minds of pupils that they are always working for results, and not merely for practice, write down the numbers from 1 to 10 in the following order:

1, 2, 5, 8, 3, 7, 4, 9, 6, 10.

Now, partly for the purpose of introducing variety into the work, and partly for the sake of review, connect both addition and subtraction with exercises in multiplication. The beginning of the work of multiplying with two may be as follows:

1 × 2 + 1 = 3.	8 × 2 − 1 = 15.	9 × 2 + 1 = .
1 × 2 − 1 = 1.	3 × 2 + 1 = .	9 × 2 − 1 = .
2 × 2 + 1 = 5.	3 × 2 − 1 = .	6 × 2 + 1 = .
2 × 2 − 1 = 3.	7 × 2 + 1 = .	6 × 2 − 1 = .
5 × 2 + 1 = 11.	7 × 2 − 1 = .	10 × 2 + 1 = .
5 × 2 − 1 = 9.	4 × 2 + 1 = .	10 × 2 − 1 = .
8 × 2 + 1 = 17.	4 × 2 − 1 = .	

Substitute the numbers 2, 3, etc., to 10, for 1 in the above exercises, as the numbers to be added and subtracted, and you have 200 examples in multiplication by 2. Now substitute the numbers 3, 4, 5, etc., to 10, in place of 2 in the above examples, as the numbers to be multiplied, and you have 1,800 examples in multiplication. With one-half of these are connected examples in addition, and with the other half examples in subtraction.

In assigning work of this kind it is only necessary for the teacher to write or dictate one or two examples of a kind; for the pupils can readily invent the rest of the series up to 20 examples.

When the pupils are familiar with the multiplication of whole numbers, as indicated above, the multiplication of fractions may be introduced with profit. If the treatment of fractions is to be easy and pleasurable, the pupils must be made entirely familiar

$$\begin{array}{ll} 1 = \frac{2}{2}. \\ 2 = \frac{4}{2}. \\ 3 = \frac{6}{2}. \\ 4 = \frac{8}{2}. \\ 5 = \frac{10}{2}. \\ 6 = \frac{12}{2}. \\ 7 = \frac{14}{2}. \\ 8 = \frac{16}{2}. \\ 9 = \frac{18}{2}. \\ 10 = \frac{20}{2}. \end{array}$$

with fractions themselves, as well as with the mode of expressing them; and for this purpose the application of the multiplication table furnishes an excellent opportunity. We will begin with the representation and multiplication of halves.

That one whole is equal to two halves may be illustrated by the actual division of a piece of paper, an apple, etc., into two equal parts. Then the same may be illustrated by dividing a line or a circle. As a result of the treatment of lines and circles in this way, the preceding work will appear on the board and on the pupils' slates.

It is only necessary to tell the pupils that half is written thus, $\frac{1}{2}$, and that the number of halves is shown by the figure above the line. The method of writing fractions needs much practice on the slates.

When the children have become familiar with the meaning and representation of halves, they may perform the following series of examples:

$1 + \frac{1}{2} = \frac{3}{2}.$ $\quad 8 - \frac{1}{2} =$ $\quad 9 + \frac{1}{2} =$
$1 - \frac{1}{2} = \frac{1}{2}.$ $\quad 3 + \frac{1}{2} =$ $\quad 9 - \frac{1}{2} =$
$2 + \frac{1}{2} = \frac{5}{2}.$ $\quad 3 - \frac{1}{2} =$ $\quad 6 + \frac{1}{2} =$
$2 - \frac{1}{2} = \frac{3}{2}.$ $\quad 7 + \frac{1}{2} =$ $\quad 6 - \frac{1}{2} =$
$5 + \frac{1}{2} =$ $\quad 7 - \frac{1}{2} =$ $\quad 10 + \frac{1}{2} =$
$5 - \frac{1}{2} =$ $\quad 4 + \frac{1}{2} =$ $\quad 10 - \frac{1}{2} =$
$8 + \frac{1}{2} =$ $\quad 4 - \frac{1}{2} =$

These exercises may be increased to almost any extent by adding and subtracting more than $\frac{1}{2}$.

A preparation for division may be made by orally questioning the children in this way: How many whole ones in $\frac{10}{2}$? How many whole ones and halves in $\frac{15}{2}$?

In a similar manner may thirds, fourths, etc., to tenths, be treated.

23. CONSTRUCTING THE TABLE.

The practice of beginning the work in multiplication by committing to memory a ready-made multiplication table cannot be too strongly condemned. But if the pupil writes down the facts in tabular form as fast as he learns them, he will construct for himself the following table, designated as Chart XIII. This will not only serve to recall the facts, but will, at the same time, be a means of teaching the facts intuitively.

CHART XIII.

1	2	3	4	5	6	7	8	9	10
2	4	6	8	10	12	14	16	18	20
3	6	9	12	15	18	21	24	27	30
4	8	12	16	20	24	28	32	36	40
5	10	15	20	25	30	35	40	45	50
6	12	18	24	30	36	42	48	54	60
7	14	21	28	35	42	49	56	63	70
8	16	24	32	40	48	56	64	72	80
9	18	27	36	45	54	63	72	81	90
10	20	30	40	50	60	70	80	90	100

That five times four are twenty may be shown thus: Count down the chart at the left to 4; there are four rectangles; at the right of these are four;

and so on to the row beginning with 5 in the upper row. That is, 5 fours are 20. If now we count the rectangles along the top row from 1 to 5, we find five in the row; below these is another row of five; and so on to the row beginning with 4 in the left-hand column. That is, four fives are 20.

In this way we obtain an intuitive knowledge that 5 fours are 20 and that 4 fives are 20. In the same way all the facts of the multiplication table may be demonstrated. Such demonstration will lay the foundation for the fact, to be learned by and by, that the product is not affected by the order of the factors.

This table is well fitted to teach the resolution of numbers into their factors; for if the children know that

$6 \times 4 = 24$,	They	$24 = 6 \times 4$;
$4 \times 6 = 24$,	must	$24 = 4 \times 6$;
$3 \times 8 = 24$,	also	$24 = 3 \times 8$;
$8 \times 3 = 24$,	know that	$24 = 8 \times 3$;

and every fact in multiplication should be followed by the corresponding fact in factoring. This is an excellent preparation for division. So also is the changing of fractions to whole numbers; for example: $\frac{9}{2} = 4$ and $\frac{1}{2}$; $\frac{17}{3} = 5$ and $\frac{2}{3}$.

In order to prepare the pupils for the work of multiplication when dealing with larger numbers, they should here be taught to multiply numbers consisting of tens and units. The following are illustrations of the work:

3 × 24 = .	4 × 18 = .	8 × 12 = .
3 × 20 = 60.	4 × 10 = 40.	8 × 10 = 80.
3 × 4 = 12.	4 × 8 = 32.	8 × 2 = 16.
3 × 24 = 72.	4 × 18 = 72.	8 × 12 = 96.

The written work in multiplication at this stage is limited. We can, however, use the following series of numbers from Chart XII.:

a, *b*, *c*, *d* by 2;   *a*, *b* by 5;   *a* by 8;
a, *b*, *c*   by 3;   *a*, *b* by 6;   *a* by 9;
a, *b*   by 4;   *a*   by 7;   *a* by 10.

In what precedes we have shown how, through objective illustrations, the products of numbers 2, 3, etc., to 10, may be understood by children, and how these products may be fixed in their minds by oral and written exercises. These products form the so-called multiplication table, by the help of which many arithmetical operations, which might be performed by the repeated addition of the same number, may be materially shortened. While constructing this table the pupil has found that the multiplication of a number is finding the sum obtained by additions of the same number. He has himself found the product by the addition of the same number; and he can in the same way find it again, should it escape his memory. But facility in computation requires that these products be made things of the memory. Remembering how to find a product is to be distinguished from remembering the product itself. In a subject like arithmetic, where the understanding is constantly called into exercise, there must be no halting of the memory. Hence we seek to make the facts of the multiplication table so appropriated by the mind that they will seem to be the necessary qualities of the memory itself. This is to be accomplished through continuous practice in computation, provision for which has been made in what precedes.

24. Preparation for Division.

It is well so to treat the subject of multiplication as to prepare the pupils for division. We have been finding products when we knew the factors; but the process is to be reversed, and we are to find the factors when the product is given; or, we are to find one factor when the product and the other factor is given. To divide 24 objects, beans, sticks, etc., into 4 equal parts, put first one object in each of 4 different places, then distribute 4 more in the same way, then 4 more, and so on till the 24 are all distributed. We now have 6 objects in each place. One of the four parts, which together contain 24 objects, contains 6 objects. It follows that 24 is 4 times 6, and also that the fourth part, or $\frac{1}{4}$, of 24 is 6.

This finding of the second factor is accomplished through successive subtractions of the same number; but facility in reckoning requires the pupil to be able, given the product and one factor, to know the other instantly. He must be taught to perform a process the opposite to what is required in finding the product from the factors. He must be able to tell at once how large a certain part of a number is, how often a certain number can be taken from another, or how often a certain number is contained in another.

Much may be done in connection with multiplication to prepare the student for such work. The following figure

```
•  •  •  •  •  •
•  •  •  •  •  •
•  •  •  •  •  •
•  •  •  •  •  •
```

illustrates these truths:

4 times 6 = 24;   6 times 4 = 24;
¼ of 24 = 6;   ⅙ of 24 = 4;
4 in 24 = 6 times;   6 in 24 = 4 times.

Therefore, to the usual questions, How many are 4 times 6? etc., add: From what number can 4 sixes be taken? 6 fours? From what number can 4 be taken 6 times? Six 4 times? In what number is 4 contained 6 times? Six 4 times? What is the fourth part of 24? The sixth? Of what number is 6 the fourth part? Four the sixth part?

If 4 apples cost 24 cents, how much will 1 cost? If 6 cost 24 cents, what costs 1? Charles stands 24 soldiers in 4 rows; how many stand in 1 row? What part of 24 is one row? 24 is how many times 6? How many times 4? etc.

If such questions as these are asked in connection with the development and application of the multiplication table, a good preparation will be made for the next stage of the work, namely, division.

25. DIVISION.

There are two kinds of division, namely, separating a number into equal parts, and finding how often one number is contained in another. As an example of the first kind, suppose 6 children have 48 cents, and the question is, How many cents will each child have, if the cents are equally divided among them? We reason that each child will have one-sixth of 48 cents, or 8 cents. Here is an actual division, a separation of the 48 cents into 6 equal parts.

As an example of the second kind of division, let the question be, Among how many children can 48 cents be divided if each child receives 6 cents? We reason thus: From 48 cents 6 cents apiece can be given to as many children as the times that 6 cents can be taken from 48 cents, or the times that 6 cents are contained in 48 cents, namely, 8 times; hence, among 8 children. Here we have found how many times 6 cents are contained in 48 cents.

In both of these examples the number 48 is divided into 6 equal parts; but while the answer to the first question is 8 cents, the answer to the second is 8 children. From these examples it appears that the solution should always correspond to the question. A confusion of the ideas involved in these two processes is a sign of a thoughtless solution. The teacher should guard against this confusion from the first, and never allow such solutions as the following:

1. If 48 cents are divided equally among 6 children, each child will receive as many cents as 6 is contained in 48. Six children are not contained in 48 cents. Here 6, that is, 6 cents, is contained in 48, that is, 48 cents, 8 times, and not 8 cents; and the comparison is really between the number of cents and the number of times that 48 contains 6. A better solution would be this: Each child would receive one-sixth of 48 cents, or 8 cents.

2. Among how many children can 48 cents be divided, if each child receives 6 cents? One-sixth part of 48 is 8; therefore, 8 children. But 48 was 48 cents, and not 48 children. A better solution would be this: If each child receives 6 cents, 48 cents could be divided among as many children as the times that 6 cents could be taken from 48 cents, namely, 8 times: hence, among 8 children.

Both forms of division must be made clear to the pupils through practical problems; for both forms are of equal use.

Division, as soon as it deals with numbers beyond the multiplication table, is a very complicated process; hence it is necessary to be very patient in teaching it, and to proceed very gradually from the easier to the more difficult. If the first difficulties are really overcome, much has been done to lighten the subsequent work.

26. Dividing by Two.

FIRST EXERCISE.

Let the children add 2 successively to 2, 4, etc., so as to form the numbers 2, 4, 6, 8, 10, etc., to 20.

Question thus? How many are 2×2? 3×2? etc. Two in 2 how many times? In 4? In 6? etc. How many times can 2 be taken from 2? From 4? etc. How many twos in 2? In 4? etc.

Give this question: Two children are to divide 12 cents equally; how many will each child receive?

Although the children are prepared, from what they have already learned, to answer this and similar questions, yet, partly to prepare them for the succeeding stage, and partly to show the teacher by an example how to manage when the difficulties involved appear in a new place, we will explain the process of working. In this example the teacher may use the cents themselves first, then marks upon the board. The latter may be arranged as those below. Having written A and B, place first a circle for a cent which A is to take, then under it one for a cent which B takes, and so on till the 12 are represented.

A. ○ ○ ○ ○ ○ ○
B. ○ ○ ○ ○ ○ ○

Each has taken 6 cents. When a number is divided into 2 equal parts, each part is a half. The half of 12 cents is 6 cents; the half of 12 is 6.

In the same way develop the idea of the half of 2, 4, 6, 8, 10, 12, 14, 16, 18, 20.

SECOND EXERCISE.

Two children have 15 apples, how many has each?

Of 14 apples each has 7 apples;
" 1 apple " " $\frac{1}{2}$ apple.
" 15 apples " " $7\frac{1}{2}$ apples.

In the same way treat 3, 5, 7, 9, 11, 13, 15, 17, and 19.

THIRD EXERCISE.

Draw on the board two rows of circles with 10 circles in each row. This will show that half of 2 rows is 1 row; half of 2 tens is 1 ten; half of 20 is 10.

In the same way may the idea of half of 20, 40, 60, 80, and 100 be developed.

The numbers 2, 4, 6, 8, 10, 12, 14, 16, 18, 20, 40, 60, 80, and 100 can be divided immediately, that is, without being separated into parts, because they appear in the twos of the multiplication table, if we regard 20, 40, etc., as 2 tens, 4 tens, etc. Numbers which do not so appear must be separated.

FOURTH EXERCISE.

Two persons together have 4 ten-cent pieces and 8 cents; how shall they divide them?

Each person takes 2 dimes and 4 cents, equal to 24 cents; so half of 48 is 24.

Or the teacher may write on the board 4 rows of 10 circles each, and 8 circles. Half of 4 rows is 2 rows; half of 8 circles is 4 circles; half of 4 tens is 2 tens; half of 40 is 20; half of 8 is 4; therefore, half of 48 is 24.

So may be developed the idea of half of those numbers whose tens and units are even numbers— 22, 24, 26, 28; 42, 44, 46, 48; 62, 64, 66, 68; 82, 84, 86, 88.

FIFTH EXERCISE.

Two persons have 3 dimes; how can they be divided? Each takes 1 dime, equal to 10 cents. They then exchange the other dime for 10 cents, and each takes 5 cents; so that each has 15 cents.

Or the teacher may draw on the board 3 rows of 10 circles each. Half of 2 rows, or 20, is 10; and half of the other row is 5; so that the half of 30 is 15.

Treat 50, 70, and 90 in the same way.

SIXTH EXERCISE.

Show on the numeral frame 3 rows of 10 balls each, and 1 row of 6 balls. What is half of them?

Half of 2 tens is 1 ten, and the other ten balls

added to the 6 make 16 balls. Half of 16 is 8; so half of 36 is 1 ten and 8, or 18.

Or this: Divide 3 dimes and 6 cents equally between two persons. Let each take 1 dime; exchange the other dime for 10 cents, which added to 6 cents make 16 cents. Let each take 8 cents, which with the dime make 18 cents.

So treat 32, 34, 36, 38; 52, 54, etc.; 72, 74, etc.; 92, 94, etc.

SEVENTH EXERCISE.

What is half of 49 apples?

<pre>
         Half of 40 apples is 20 apples;
          "   8   "   4 apples;
          "   1   "   ½ apple.
                           ─────────
          "   49 apples is 24½ apples.
</pre>

So treat all numbers which have even tens and odd units: 21, 23, 25, 27, 29; 41, 43, 45, 47, 49; 61, 63, etc.; 81, 83, etc.

EIGHTH EXERCISE.

What is half of 57?

<pre>
        Half of 40 is 20;
         "   16 "   8;
         "   1 "   ½.
                      ─────
         "   57 " 28½.
</pre>

Treat in the same way all numbers whose tens and units are odd numbers: 33, 35, 37, 39; 53, 55, etc.; 73, 75, etc.; 93, 95, etc.

ILLUSTRATIVE EXAMPLES.

We will show by an example of the last exercise (exercise eight) what the full treatment of a problem in division should be, as it has been developed in the successive stages of work in division. Division requires a series of conclusions, and in this fact lies the difficulty which it presents to the children. There is no cause for discouragement, however; for if division by 2 is thoroughly mastered, the remaining numbers can be passed over much more rapidly. Do not introduce the children to the formal, written representation of the process till they have attained considerable facility in explaining it. If they need to be occupied with written work, there is material enough in the review of what precedes, — especially in addition, subtraction, and multiplication. Probably it will take from four to six weeks to ground a class thoroughly in division of numbers below 100 by 2. Division by the numbers from 3 to 10 will scarcely require more time. The successive steps in the solution of a question in the division of a number by 2 when both the tens and units are odd numbers may be brought out thus:

(1) *Teacher.* We will find the half of 75. Can we divide 75 immediately; that is, all at once?

Scholar. We cannot divide 75 immediately.

(2) *T.* Why not?

S. Because 75 is not found in the twos of the multiplication table.

(3) *T.* Can we divide 7 tens immediately?

S. We cannot divide 7 tens immediately.

(4) *T.* Why not?

S. Because 7 is not found in the twos of the multiplication table.

(5) *T.* What is the next number below 7 that is found there?

S. Six is the next number.

(6) *T.* What is the half of 6 tens, or 60?

S. Half of 6 tens, or 60, is 3 tens, or 30.

(7) *T.* How many of 75 remain to be divided when we have divided 60?

S. Fifteen remain to be divided.

(8) *T.* Can we divide 15 immediately?

S. We cannot divide 15 immediately.

(9) *T.* Why not?

S. Because 15 is not found in the twos of the multiplication table.

(10) *T.* What is the next number below 15 that is found there?

S. Fourteen is the next number.

(11) *T.* What is half of 14?

S. Half of 14 is 7.

(12) *T.* How many still remain to be divided?

S. One still remains to be divided.

(13) *T.* What is half of 1?

S. One-half is half of 1.

(14) *T.* How many did we at first obtain, when we divided 60?

S. We at first obtained 30.
(15) *T.* Then how many?
S. Then 7.
(16) *T.* Then?
S. One-half.
(17) *T.* Add them all together.
S. $30 + 7 + \frac{1}{2} = 37\frac{1}{2}$.
(18) *T.* Give the entire solution.
S. What is half of 75?

$$\begin{aligned} \text{Half of } 60 &= 30. \\ \text{Half of } 14 &= 7. \\ \text{Half of } 1 &= \tfrac{1}{2}. \\ \hline \text{Half of } 75 &= 37\tfrac{1}{2}. \end{aligned}$$

This example will be sufficient to show how complicated is the process of division, and how very nicely the work should be graded, so as to lead the pupils to ask and answer by themselves all the necessary questions. At first the teacher asks the questions; but soon the brighter pupils may act as teachers. They may take their places in turn before the class, and question their fellow pupils. This must be continued till all, even the dull ones, are able to do the same. The brightest children may be set to questioning single rows or small divisions. Gradually the pupils will begin to unite the several successive processes; at first two, and finally all. It is the same here as in other complex mental processes: at first we perform the successive steps consciously;

and then, as they are repeated, we seem to omit more or less of the intervening steps and to reach the conclusion at once. To make this result possible, however, it is absolutely necessary that each step be not only expressed but understood. Hence the importance of thorough illustration and also of well-graded and abundant practice.

When the pupil has been through all the work in division of numbers by 2 which has now been pointed out, so that he is prepared independently to arrange the conclusions in order, he may be put at written work. The form of this may be the following:

$\frac{1}{2}$ of 75.	2 in 75.
$\frac{1}{2}$ of 60 = 30.	2 in 60 = 30 times.
$\frac{1}{2}$ of 14 = 7.	2 in 14 = 7 times.
$\frac{1}{2}$ of 1 = $\frac{1}{2}$.	2 in 1 = $\frac{1}{2}$ times.
$\frac{1}{2}$ of 75 = 37$\frac{1}{2}$.	2 in 75 = 37$\frac{1}{2}$ times.

Such work as this is the best preparation for the division of larger numbers; but then the written form must be the result of a thorough comprehension. It is of importance that every figure stands in its proper place. For this purpose it is well to divide the slates into little rectangles, and to have one figure put in each. The written solution of a problem should be a picture of order. The orderly arrangement of the work makes it possible to dispense with many words; it tends to mathematical brevity and definiteness; and it materially shortens the teacher's work of correction.

If the division of small mumbers is to be a preparation for the division of larger numbers, the forms which represent the two processes should agree. The arrangement of the written work, in case of large numbers, is the following:

$$2 \overline{)75} (37\tfrac{1}{2}$$
$$\frac{6}{15}$$
$$\frac{14}{1}$$

The separation of the dividend into parts, in the form given above, is sufficiently like this to give no trouble in later work; but any other separation — as into 70, 4, and 1, or into 72, 2, and 1, because the children happen to know the half of these numbers — would be wrong practice, because it would not be a preparation for higher work; for in the division of large numbers the result is to be reached figure by figure, and hence the same should be true in the division of small numbers. The experienced arithmetician, especially when his work is wholly mental, is bound by no rules. He often reaches the result by a short cut. But it is never to be lost sight of that it is the business of this stage of the work to develop the power of arithmetical calculation. It will be time enough later to teach shorthand processes.

Then, too, the importance of performing the work

at one stage in such a way as to prepare the pupils for subsequent stages is too often overlooked. It is much easier to make children comprehend the processes of division, as they stand related to one another, when dealing with numbers completely within their comprehension than in the treatment of incomprehensible numbers; hence the importance of slow and well-graded progress in division of small numbers by 2.

The young teacher should not be impatient if much time is spent with the number 2; for if the fundamental conceptions of division are here made clear, subsequent progress will not only be more rapid, but much freer from that confusion which results from an attempt to teach a new principle in connection with indistinctly formed ideas.

27. Dividing by Three.

First develop through illustrations — as, for example, balls on the numeral frame, sticks, buttons, or marks of various kinds on the board — the third part of 3, 6, 9, 12, 15, 18, 21, 24, 27, 30, 60, 90; then the third part of 1 and 2. The latter may be done by dividing a piece of paper into 3 equal parts, and naming each part $\frac{1}{3}$; then by treating a second piece in the same way. A practical problem may be used for the same purpose: three children have 2 apples to divide among them; what part does each receive?

They cut one apple into 3 equal parts, and each takes 1 part, or ⅓ of an apple. They then treat the second in the same way. Each child then has ⅔ of an apple; so ⅓ of 2 apples is ⅔ of 1 apple. Or, lay two equal circles of paper one upon the other, and cut them into 3 equal parts. Each double part is ⅓ of the 2 pieces, or ⅔ of 1 piece.

In the development of the process of dividing by 3 it will not be necessary to divide the work into stages so carefully graded as in the treatment of division by 2. I will, however, indicate the corresponding stages, as they are always useful in the treatment of dull pupils. They are the following:

a. 3, 6, 9, 12, 15, 18, 21, 24, 27, 30, 60, 90.
b. 1, 4, 7, 10, 13, 16, 19, 22, 25, 28.
c. 2, 5, 8, 11, 14, 17, 20, 23, 26, 29.
d. 33, 36, 39, 63, 66, 69, 93, 96, 99.
e. 42, 45, 48, 51, 54, 57, 72, 75, 78, 81, 84, 87.
f. The rest of the numbers below 100.

An example will show the agreement of the treatment with that of dividing by 2.

Three boys are to divide 89 cents among them; they have 8 dimes and 9 cents. How many cents does each receive?

Teacher. How many dimes can each take?
Scholar. Each can take 2 dimes.
T. What will be left?
S. 2 dimes and 9 cents = 29 cents.

T. Can they divide 29 cents at once?

S. No, for 29 is not found in the threes of the multiplication table.

T. What is the next number below 29 that is found there?

S. 27 is the next number.

T. What is a third of 27?

S. 9 is a third of 27.

T. How many cents has each now?

S. $20 + 9 = 29$.

T. How many cents are still to be divided?

S. 2 cents.

T. How much does each receive of 2 cents?

S. $\frac{2}{3}$ of a cent.

T. How many cents has each altogether?

S. $20 + 9 + \frac{2}{3} = 29\frac{2}{3}$.

The pupil must finally be brought to the point where he can give the following solution in substance alone:

We cannot divide 89 immediately by 3, because it is not found in the threes of the multiplication table. The next number found there below 89 is 60. A third of $60 = 20$. Now 29 remains to be divided. As 29 is not in the threes of the multiplication table, we divide the next lower number, 27. A third of 27 is 9. We have now divided 87, and 2 remains to be divided. A third of $2 = \frac{2}{3}$. So that the third part of $89 = 20 + 9 + \frac{2}{3} = 29\frac{2}{3}$.

Written exercises in dividing by 3 are not to be assigned to the pupils till they have gained a thorough understanding of the matter and some facility in solving problems. The written expression for the example just given will appear as follows:

$\frac{1}{3}$ of 89.		3 in 89.
$\frac{1}{3}$ of 60 = 20.		3 in 60 = 20 times.
$\frac{1}{3}$ of 27 = 9.	or,	3 in 27 = 9 times.
$\frac{1}{3}$ of 2 = $\frac{2}{3}$.		3 in 2 = $\frac{2}{3}$ times.
$\frac{1}{3}$ of 89 = 29$\frac{2}{3}$.		3 in 89 = 29$\frac{2}{3}$ times.

Which form is to be used will depend upon the special statement of the question and its solution.

28. Dividing by Other Numbers to 10.

After the treatment of division by 2 and 3 it will not be necessary to go into particulars in regard to dividing by 4, 5, 6, 7, 8, 9, and 10. The same method is to be followed with all these numbers. When they have all been taught, the pupils may be required, by way of review, to divide a number by each of the fundamental numbers in turn. Great facility should be attained in the division of those numbers which are of special importance in business; as, 12, 24, 25, 30, 50, 60, 100.

It will be observed that division, as indicated above, depends upon the separation of numbers into tens and units, although the words tens and units have been for the most part avoided. Let us divide 89 by three, using these terms:

89 consists of 8 tens and 9 units. A third of 8 tens is 2 tens, with a remainder of 2 tens, which are equal to 20 units. Add 9 units and the sum is 29 units. A third of 29 units is 9 units, with a remainder of 2 units. A third part of 2 units is $\frac{2}{3}$. Hence, $\frac{1}{3}$ of $89 = 2$ tens $+ 9$ units $+ \frac{2}{3} = 29\frac{2}{3}$.

This solution requires more statements than the one given above; and there is danger that some of these may escape the memory. Frequently the process is shorter if the number to be divided is separated into the parts indicated in the first solution; as, $89 = 60 + 27 + 2$. The separating of numbers in this way is the most important part of division.

29. Practice Work.

In the preceding work on division it must appear that there is a necessity for the most careful separation of the work into stages founded upon the degree of difficulties to be overcome; so that the work will conform to the educational maxim: From the easier to the more difficult. First come the numbers found within the multiplication table; then follow those without this table, but divisible without a remainder; and finally, those numbers which lie beyond the table, but are not divisible without a remainder.

Some of the work in the division of numbers below

a hundred is no doubt more difficult than work with numbers between 100 and 1,000; and yet these are fundamental difficulties, and it is better to conquer them in connection with small numbers.

In some cases, however, it may be well to limit the division of numbers at this stage, and not apply it to all numbers. The following is a good selection of numbers for this purpose:

By 2 divide numbers from 1 to 20.
" 3 " " " 1 " 30.
" 4 " " " 1 " 40.
" 5 " " " 1 " 50.
" 6 " " " 1 " 60.
" 7 " " " 1 " 70.
" 8 " " " 1 " 80.
" 9 " " " 1 " 90.
" 10 " " " 1 " 100.

Chart XII. will be found useful at this stage, because it contains all numbers below 100, so arranged that they can be readily assigned for practice in division:

By 2, series a, b.
" 3, " a, b, c.
" 4, " a, b, c, d.
" 5, " a, b, c, d, e.
" 6, " a, b, c, d, e, f.
" 7, " a, b, c, d, e, f, g.
" 8, " a, b, c, d, e, f, g, h.
" 9, " $a, b, c, d, e, f, g, h, i$.
" 10, " $a, b, c, d, e, f, g, h, i, k$.

The number 100 should receive special consideration at this time. One kind of exercises is the finding of every two parts of which 100 consists; for example:

99 + 1, 98 + 2, 97 + 3, 96 + 4, 95 + 5,
94 + 6, 93 + 7, 92 + 8, 91 + 9, 90 + 10,
89 + 11, and so on to 50 + 50.

Another kind of exercises is the following: 100 is equal to

1 × 100, 2 × 50, 3 × 33 + 1, 4 × 25,
5 × 20, 6 × 16 + 4, 7 × 14 + 2, 8 × 12 + 4,
and so on to 50 × 2.

A third kind of work, which ought to be done before passing on to the treatment of numbers to 1,000, is making change from a dollar for any smaller sum; for example: 33 cents from a dollar; the change may be 2 cents, a nickel, a dime, and half a dollar, or 2 quarters.

CHAPTER IV.

NUMBERS FROM ONE TO A THOUSAND.

30. COUNTING AND WRITING.

101 to 200.

FOR the same reason that it was thought best for pupils to be made acquainted with numbers from eleven to twenty before studying numbers from twenty to one hundred, it is here recommended that they be made somewhat familiar with numbers from 101 to 200 before they are required to deal at all with numbers from 201 to 1,000. The following steps will bring the pupils to the desired result:

1. Counting from 101 to 200.
2. Counting from 200 to 101.
3. Writing numbers from 101 to 200.
4. Reading numbers written on the board by the teacher.
5. Writing the numbers from dictation.
6. Separating the numbers from 101 to 200, into

a. Hundreds, tens, and units, as, for example:

   134 = 1 hundreds, 3 tens, and 4 units.
   150 = 1   "   5 "   " 0   "
   105 = 1   "   0 "   " 5   "
   200 = 2   "   0 "   " 0   "

b. Tens and units, as, for example:

$$134 = 13 \text{ tens, and } 4 \text{ units.}$$
$$150 = 15 \text{ `` `` } 0 \text{ ``}$$
$$105 = 10 \text{ `` `` } 5 \text{ ``}$$
$$200 = 20 \text{ `` `` } 0 \text{ ``}$$

If the work on numbers below one hundred has been thoroughly done, there will be need of but little objective teaching at this stage of the work. It would be well for the teacher to be provided with a few strings of one hundred buttons each, or a few bunches of sticks, each bunch containing one hundred; so that he can illustrate his work objectively, and afford an opportunity for the dull pupils to handle the objects themselves. But it is by no means necessary to present all the numbers at this stage of the work in the form of objects in the hands of every child. Too much objective teaching of numbers is only less stultifying than too little. It is now time to appeal to the imagination and to the power of abstraction.

201 to 1,000.

The pupils should now be taught to count by hundreds to 1,000; then the numbers 201, etc., to 1,000 should be treated in the same way, and by the same steps as were recommended in the case of numbers from 101 to 200, including the separation of the numbers into hundreds, tens, and units, as shown above under *a* and *b*.

This work of counting, reading, writing, etc., should

be continued till the pupils have clear ideas of all numbers below 1,000, know them as composed of units, tens, and hundreds, and know how their component parts are represented by figures. The test of this last item of knowledge is the ability of the pupil to select the groups of objects, and the single objects, for which the different figures of any number below 1,000 stand. When this test can be easily borne, it is time to advance to the different fundamental operations, but not before.

31. ADDITION.

The more thoroughly pupils are drilled in adding numbers expressed by two figures, that is, numbers below a hundred, the easier will be the work of learning the addition of numbers represented by three figures. Hence it is well at this point to make a thorough review of the addition of numbers below a hundred. For this purpose Chart XII. will be found very convenient. If all numbers from eleven to one hundred are in turn added to each of the numbers on the chart, the pupils will have 90 times 100, or 9,000 examples; while the teacher will be spared the labor of copying any of them on the board. The following suggestions are offered as to the proper stages of the review here recommended.

Let the pupils add the numbers written below to each of the numbers on Chart XII., proceeding from left to right:

120   ARITHMETIC IN PRIMARY SCHOOLS.

First Stage.	a 10,	b 20,	c 30,	d 40 -	- 100.
Second "	11,	21,	31,	41 -	- 91.
Third "	12,	22,	32,	42 -	- 92.
Fourth "	13,	23,	33,	43 -	- 93.
etc.	etc.	etc.	etc.	etc.	etc.

These exercises should, as far as possible, be performed orally; but, when necessary, the pupils may be required to indicate the work on their slates. Suppose it is required to add the number 47 to each of the numbers on Chart XII., the work will appear on the slate in the following order:

$1+47=48$	$76+47=123$	$43+47=90$
$12+47=59$	$84+47=131$	$52+47=99$
$26+47=73$	$96+47=143$	$70+47=117$
$34+47=81$	$2+47=49$	$73+47=120$
$47+47=94$	$19+47=66$	$87+47=134$
$53+47=100$	$22+47=69$	$93+47=140$
$67+47=114$	$31+47=78$	etc. etc. etc.

Or the pupils may be required to write the results only; then the results of the above additions would assume this form:

	a.	b.	c.	d.	e.	f.	g.	h.	i.	k.
l.	48	59	73	81	94	100	114	123	131	143
m.	49	66	69	78	90	99	117	120	134	140
n.	etc., etc.									

It will be noticed that the numbers to be added first are those consisting of tens only, then those consisting of tens and units. In adding the latter class of numbers, the tens should be added first and then the units; for example: $95+47$; $95+40=135$; $135+7=142$; hence, $95+47=142$.

The pupils should acquire considerable facility in adding numbers of two places before proceeding to the addition of larger numbers. When they are prepared to advance to work with larger numbers, they should be assigned examples in the following order:

a. Both numbers containing tens only; as,

$$40+30=70.$$
$$80+70=150.$$

b. One number containing tens and units, the other tens only; as,

$$45+30=75.$$
$$48+60=108.$$

c. Both numbers containing tens and units; as,

$$43+24=67.$$
$$86+75=161.$$

d. One number containing hundreds, tens, and units, and the other only tens and units; as,

$$238+46=284.$$
$$475+48=523.$$

e. Both numbers containing hundreds, tens, and units; as,

$$425+248=673.$$
$$436+398=834.$$

The above is the order in adding two numbers

only; the addition of columns of numbers comes later. This work is all to be done mentally before any part of the result is written. In adding two numbers, the following rule is universally to be followed:

The first number is not to be separated into parts; when the second consists of tens and units, the tens are to be added first, then the units; when it consists of hundreds, tens, and units, the hundreds are to be added first, then the tens, and lastly the units, *e.g.*:

$367 + 86$; $367 + 80 = 447$; $447 + 6 = 453$. $378 + 285$; $378 + 200 = 578$; $578 + 80 = 658$; $658 + 5 = 663$.

Only a few examples like the last should be given; and these mainly to the ablest pupils.

The pupils should have enough work like the above, on pure numbers, to make them familiar with the processes of addition; and then the knowledge and power thus gained should be applied to the solution of simple practical problems. Indeed, some practical problems should be given with almost every lesson.

32. SUBTRACTION.

Before beginning the subtraction of numbers above a hundred, the subtraction of numbers below a hundred should be thoroughly reviewed. When this has been done, a judicious use of Chart XII. will save the teacher much time and labor.

In the first stage of this work the minuend should not exceed 200. If, now, the pupil is taught to think of each number on Chart XII. as 100 larger than it is, and to use these increased numbers as minuends, each number on the Chart may be used as a subtrahend, and thus the teacher will have, ready made, 100 × 100, or 10,000, examples in subtraction.

These examples should be assigned in the following order :

a. The subtrahend containing tens only ; as,

$$101 - 20 \qquad 101 - 60$$
$$112 - 20 \qquad 112 - 60$$
$$\text{etc., etc.} \qquad \text{etc., etc.}$$

b. The subtrahend containing tens and units ; as,

$$101 - 24 \qquad 101 - 67$$
$$112 - 24 \qquad 112 - 67$$
$$\text{etc., etc.} \qquad \text{etc., etc.}$$

Any number from 201 to 1,000 may be used as a minuend, and each of the numbers on Chart XII. as a subtrahend, and thus we have 80,000 more examples in subtraction without the trouble of inventing them or writing them on the board.

These examples are all to be solved mentally. When it is desirable to have the results written down by the pupils, the written work may assume this form :

$$147 - 1 = 146 \qquad 147 - 2 = 145$$
$$147 - 12 = 135 \qquad 147 - 19 = 128$$
$$147 - 26 = 121 \qquad 147 - 22 = 125$$
$$147 - 34 = 113 \qquad 147 - 31 = 116$$
$$147 - 47 = 100 \qquad 147 - 43 = 104$$
$$\text{etc., etc., etc.} \qquad \text{etc., etc., etc.}$$

Or the work may be more briefly represented thus:

	a.	b.	c.	d.	e.	f.	g.	h.	i.	k.
l.	146	135	121	113	100	94	80	71	63	51
m.	145	128	125	116	104	95	77	74	60	54
n.	etc., etc.									

The rule for subtracting numbers consisting of units and tens, as previously given, is this: First subtract the tens, then the units; as,

$$132 - 47; \; 132 - 40 = 92; \; 92 - 7 = 85; \; \text{so } 132 - 47 = 85.$$

The brightest pupils may be encouraged to find new ways of reaching the result; for example:

$$47 = 50 - 3; \; 132 - 50 = 82; \; 82 + 3 = 85.$$
$$47 = 42 + 5; \; 132 - 42 = 90; \; 90 - 5 = 85.$$

If the work here indicated on numbers below 200 is thoroughly done, no special difficulty will be found in the subtraction of numbers between 200 and 1,000. It would be well, however, to grade the work in the following way:

a. The minuend containing hundreds and tens; the subtrahend containing tens only; as,

$$940 - 80 = 860$$
$$770 - 80 = 690$$
$$680 - 80 = 600$$
etc., etc., etc.

b. The minuend containing hundreds, tens, and units; the subtrahend containing only tens; as,

$$997 - 60 = 937$$
$$937 - 60 = 877$$
$$877 - 60 = 817$$
etc., etc., etc.

c. The minuend containing hundreds, tens, and units; the subtrahend containing tens and units; as,

$$997 - 67 = 930$$
$$930 - 67 = 863$$
$$863 - 67 = 796$$
etc., etc., etc.

d. Both minuend and subtrahend containing hundreds, tens, and units; as,

$$993 - 267 = 726.$$

In all cases the rule for the subtraction of a number consisting of units, tens, and hundreds is this: Never separate the minuend into parts; but subtract the hundreds of the subtrahend first, then the tens, and last the units; for example:

$993 - 267$; $993 - 200 = 793$; $793 - 60 = 733$; $733 - 7 = 726$.

Here the subtraction can sometimes be most easily performed by adding enough to the subtrahend to make a sum equal to the minuend; for example:

$$975 - 388.$$
$$388 + 12 = 400;$$
$$400 + 575 = 975;$$
$$575 + 12 = 587.$$

It is possible to construct drill exercises in addition and subtraction, by making the processes alternate, which will at the same time require much work on the part of the pupils and very little on the part of the teacher. Suppose the exercise set for the class to be this: Beginning with 746, alternately add 248 and subtract 273. The work would assume the following form on the slates:

$$746 + 248 = 994; \quad 994 - 273 = 721.$$
$$721 + 248 = 969; \quad 969 - 273 = 696.$$
$$696 + 248 = 944; \quad 944 - 273 = 671.$$
$$671 + 248 = 919; \quad 919 - 273 = 646.$$

The final result is just 100 less than 746, the number with which the work began. The reason is that 273, the number to be subtracted, is 25 more than 248, the number to be added, and consequently each addition and subtraction diminishes the original number 25: and four additions and subtractions diminish it just 100.

The teacher can readily construct any amount of drill work, such that the correction of slates will be as easy as in the example given; for he has only to substitute any other number for 476, and any other numbers differing from each other by 25 for 248 and 273.

This kind of examples is well adapted to furnishing every pupil, dull or bright, with all the work he can do in a given time; for the work in the problem given above, is only to be continued in order to furnish 29 examples in addition and as many in subtraction, which can be corrected at a glance.

While facility in addition and subtraction is of the greatest importance in practical business, care must be taken not to weary and discourage the pupils. Hence it is recommended that problems like those given above be not introduced too often, nor continued too long.

33. MULTIPLICATION.

Before beginning the multiplication of numbers between 100 and 1,000, the multiplication table should be thoroughly reviewed. Then should follow the multiplication of numbers between 10 and 100, which will be also partly a review. The three stages of the work will be the following:

a. MULTIPLICATION OF TENS.

$9 \times 20 = 9 \times 2$ tens $= 18$ tens $= 180$.
$9 \times 70 = 9 \times 7$ " $= 63$ " $= 630$.

The pupils are to be familiar with the changing of tens to units. Then this work of changing units to tens and of changing tens to units may be soon omitted, and the result reached at once; as,

$$9 \times 20 = 180; \ 9 \times 70 = 630.$$

b. MULTIPLICATION OF TENS AND UNITS.

$$\begin{array}{r} 6 \times 39 = \\ 6 \times 30 = 180 \\ 6 \times 9 = 54 \\ \hline 6 \times 39 = 234 \end{array}$$

The above example illustrates both the order of procedure in purely mental reckoning, and also a good order of arrangement when the results of mental operations are to be recorded.

c. MULTIPLICATION OF HUNDREDS, TENS, AND UNITS.

$2 \times 478; \ 2 \times 400 = 800; \ 2 \times 70 = 140; \ 800 + 140 = 940; \ 2 \times 8 = 16; \ 940 + 16 = 956.$

The order of multiplication is first the hundreds, then the tens, and lastly the units. In multiplying in the head, always begin with the highest order, and work towards the units. By this procedure we are compelled to repeat the partial results more than by the reverse process. Then, too, when results are to be united, they should be united as quickly as possible, so as to cause the least draught upon the memory. This applies especially to the multiplication of three-place numbers.

MULTIPLICATION.

If the numbers from 1 to 10 are written on the board in an irregular order, — as 1, 2, 5, 8, 3, 7, 4, 9, 6, 10, — problems in multiplication can be easily set for a class, and so can examples requiring either addition or subtraction to be combined with multiplication. The following will serve as suggestions both for the invention of the problems and for the arrangement of the work by the pupils:

$1 \times 70 = 70$ $\qquad$ $1 \times 36 = 36$
$2 \times 70 = 140$ $\qquad$ $2 \times 36 = 72$
$5 \times 70 = 350$ $\qquad$ $5 \times 36 = 180$
$8 \times 70 = 560$ $\qquad$ $8 \times 36 = 288$
$3 \times 70 = 210$ $\qquad$ $3 \times 36 = 108$
$7 \times 70 = 490$ $\qquad$ $7 \times 36 = 252$
$4 \times 70 = 280$ $\qquad$ $4 \times 36 = 144$
$9 \times 70 = 630$ $\qquad$ $9 \times 36 = 324$
$6 \times 70 = 420$ $\qquad$ $6 \times 36 = 216$
$10 \times 70 = 700$ $\qquad$ $10 \times 36 = 360$

$1 \times 70 + 42 =$ $\qquad$ $1 \times 36 + 27 =$
$1 \times 70 - 42 =$ $\qquad$ $1 \times 36 - 27 =$
$2 \times 70 + 42 =$ $\qquad$ $2 \times 36 + 27 =$
$2 \times 70 - 42 =$ $\qquad$ $2 \times 36 - 27 =$
$5 \times 70 + 42 =$ $\qquad$ $5 \times 36 + 27 =$
$5 \times 70 - 42 =$ $\qquad$ $5 \times 36 - 27 =$
$\qquad$ etc. $\qquad\qquad\qquad$ etc.

In performing the first of such exercises, when the results are to be written, the teacher should insist upon having the work so arranged as to show all the steps in the solution; as,

$$5 \times 36 + 27$$
$$5 \times 30 = 150$$
$$5 \times 6 = 30$$
$$\overline{5 \times 27 = 180}$$
$$\overline{180 + 27 = 207}$$

Examples of the multiplication of hundreds, tens, and units will be but few, if the product does not exceed 1,000.

Chart XIII. will furnish an abundance of examples in multiplication. The teacher may require every number on the chart to be multiplied by 1, 2, etc., to 10. Whatever tends to lessen the labor of the teacher without injuring the quality of his work is not to be despised.

It is well, at this stage of the work, to extend the pupils' knowledge of the multiplication table to 11 and 12. For ordinary students it is hardly worth while to go beyond 12.

After the pupils have been well drilled in the multiplication of pure numbers, special attention should be given to the solution of practical problems. It will be necessary for the teacher to assist the pupils in the study of these problems. He will also have an excellent opportunity to impart much practical information in regard to those matters to which the problems refer, and to drill the pupils in the expression and application of the numerical ideas which they have already acquired, and of the practical truths which he imparts. In the solution of such problems the pupils necessarily receive continuous drill in sustained trains of reasoning. The following is an example:

If beans are sold at 12 cents a quart, or 80 cents a peck, how much is saved by buying a peck all at once rather than by the single quart?

If one quart costs 12 cents, a peck, or 8 quarts, would cost 8 × 12 cents, or 96 cents; and 96 cents are 16 cents more than 80 cents; therefore 16 cents would be saved by buying a peck at a time.

The study of a problem of this kind gives the teacher an opportunity to impart to the pupils some elementary ideas upon wholesale and retail trade, as well as upon domestic economy; while the pupil is exercised in the expression of the relation of numbers, and also in going through a train of connected reasoning and its expression.

The development of the reasoning power in connection with the learning of arithmetic is too often undervalued. Arithmetic does not mean simply producing one number from another by adding and subtracting, multiplying and dividing; but, rather, judging, thinking, reasoning. Operations with numbers can be introduced only after conclusions are reached through the power of thought. A practical arithmetician is not a man who has attained great skill simply in uniting numbers to form new numbers, skill in numerical operations; but rather one who knows how, as well, to make the judgments necessary to be used in the solution of practical problems. If a person wishes to make others understand what he himself has clearly thought out, he must take pains to set it out in clear words and sentences. If instruction in arithmetic is to result in something more than mechanical skill in numerical operations, the pupil must be practised, at every stage of the work, both in performing the steps of the reasoning processes required in the solution of problems and also in the brief, exact, and definite verbal expression of such reasoning. However valuable mechanical skill in performing operations upon numbers may be, it is of only secondary importance. Of much more importance is the ability to perform the reasoning processes which lead to the solution of practical problems. This reasoning discovers the numerical operations necessary for reaching the desired result; and without the reasoning the operations could not be performed.

34. Division.

Before beginning the division of numbers between 1 and 1,000, a careful review of the division of numbers from 1 to 100 should be made; for the teacher cannot too often remember that the new is always to be united with the old.

DIVISION.

DIVIDING BY TWO.

The first thing to be done here is to make clear to the children, and then give them ample practice in finding, the half

a. Of 2, 4, 6, 8, 10, 12, 14, 16, 18, — units.
b. Of 20, 40, 60, 80, 100, 120, 140, 160, 180, — tens.
c. Of 200, 400, 600, 800, 1,000, — hundreds.

This done, the following problem and solution will show the proper treatment of numbers which should follow:

Divide 573 by two.

The number 573 consists of 5 hundreds, 7 tens, and 3 units. We must first divide four of the five hundreds; half of 4 hundreds is 2 hundreds = 200.
1 hundred = 10 tens; 10 tens and 7 tens make 17 tens. Half of 16 tens is 8 tens 80
One ten remains, equal to 10 units; to which add 3 units, and we have 13 units. Half of 12 units = ... 6
Half of 1 = ... $\frac{1}{2}$
Half of 573 = 286$\frac{1}{2}$

In order to bring the pupils to the point of facility in the strictly mental division of numbers from 1 to 1,000, it is necessary for them to use the greatest brevity of thought and expression; hence they should soon be taught to separate the number to be divided into divisible parts without the use of the words "hundreds," "tens," and "units." The written expression of the work given above will then assume the following form :

$\frac{1}{2}$ of 573 =
$\frac{1}{2}$ of 400 = 200
$\frac{1}{2}$ of 160 = 80
$\frac{1}{2}$ of 12 = 6
$\frac{1}{2}$ of 1 = $\frac{1}{2}$
───────────────
$\frac{1}{2}$ of 573 = 286$\frac{1}{2}$

From the preceding we derive the following : First divide the hundreds which are divisible without a remainder; reduce the hundreds which cannot be directly divided to tens, and to these add the tens; divide what of the tens can be divided without a remainder ; reduce the rest of the tens to units, and to these add the units, etc.

The following figures will show how thoroughly the foregoing work prepares the pupils for the usual written form of division :

$$573 \div 2 = 286\frac{1}{2}$$
4 . .
───
17 . .
16 .
───
13
12
───
1

After the detailed explanation in regard to division

of numbers from 1 to 100, it must be unnecessary to go further into detail here. If the practice there recommended is here reviewed, the pupils will now generally find no difficulty in dividing numbers below 1,000 by 3, 4, 5, 6, 7, 8, 9, 10, or by 20, 30, 40, etc., to 100. It will sometimes happen, however, that children will come from an unskilful teacher, or will be generally so dull that it will be desirable, at this stage, to introduce division first by 2, then by 3, etc., to 10, and to drill on each number by itself. In such case, it is recommended that the divisible hundreds, tens, and units be treated at first by themselves; for example, the division, by 3, of

a. 3, 6, 9, 12, 15, 18, — units;
b. 30, 60, 90, 120, 150, 180, — tens;
c. 300, 600, 900, — hundreds.

So may the division by the other units be introduced, and frequently with profit.

Practical problems are necessarily omitted in these papers: but they are by no means to be omitted from the pupils' work. The young teacher is earnestly recommended to make use of books of problems, and not to rely solely upon his power of invention. Such books should be used a part of the time by the pupils themselves. In this way the power of reading and of interpreting the written page is developed. A part of the time the problems should be read to the pupils by the teacher. If, now, the teacher adopts the invariable practice of reading a problem but once, the pupils' power of attention will be greatly strengthened.

The material for mental work in all the fundamental rules can be indefinitely increased by the use of Chart XIII., as has been explained heretofore. The pupils can use it as the basis of thousands of examples to be performed in school upon the slate, which take the place of mental work without the slate. More of such exercises in the fundamental rules will now be suggested.

ADDITION.

To 365 add each number on Chart XIII. That gives 100 problems in addition. Now, instead of 365, each number from 101 to 1,000 may be used; which gives $900 \times 100 = 90,000$ additions.

The correctness of the results may be proved at the end of the hour by letting the pupils change slates and read the answers through.

SUBTRACTION.

Let each number on Chart XIII. be subtracted from 365. Then, in place of 365, use each number from 101 to 1,000, and we have, in all, $900 \times 100 = 90,000$ subtractions.

MULTIPLICATION.

Multiply each number on the chart by 2, 3, 4, etc., to 12, and we have 1,100 multiplications. Write 1, 2,

3, 4, etc., to 12, before each number on the chart, and multiply by 2, 3, 4, etc., to 12, and we have 121,000 multiplications.

DIVISION.

Put the figure 1 before each number of the chart, and divide the resulting number by 2, 3, 4, etc., to 12, and there are 1,100 divisions. Replace the 1 by 3, 4, 5, etc., to 12, successively, and we have $11 \times 1,100 = 12,100$ divisions.

The ingenious teacher will be able to save time and labor in other ways by the use of this chart.

35. Written and Mental Arithmetic.

Heretofore written and mental arithmetic have not been separated. The form of the written exercises has corresponded strictly to the course of thought in the mental exercises. It is possible, however, to manage the written work in such a way as to save both space and time. But, although this saving is important, it is not to be gained at the expense of clear understanding. The mind of the learner needs to be prepared beforehand for obtaining a clear insight into the reasons for the shorter processes of written work, which are of special advantage in dealing with larger numbers; and on this account their consideration has been postponed to a later stage.

Sometimes the terms mental arithmetic and written arithmetic are set over against each other, as though they stood for two distinct kinds of arithmetical work. Such a division, however, is incorrect; for all arithmetical computation is made by the mind. The use of the terms oral arithmetic and memory arithmetic on the one hand, and of slate arithmetic and figuring or ciphering on the other, is often faulty for the same reason.

It is true that sometimes figures are used to assist the memory in retaining the numbers under consideration, and at others the work is done by the mind without such help; and perhaps no better terms have been invented to indicate these two facts than the old names of written and mental arithmetic. It is certain that the use of no other terms would change the facts, or make the two processes either more or less alike.

What problems belong to written arithmetic and what ones to mental arithmetic depends upon the ability of the pupils to hold in the memory more or fewer, larger or smaller numbers. Then, too, a pupil well drilled in mental arithmetic will often solve problems without the use of figures, when others would require the aid of pen or pencil. There can no absolute limit to either class of problems be drawn. In general, however, it is sufficient if the problems of ordinary business, which do not involve numbers larger than a thousand, can be solved without the aid of figures; though, of course, problems may sometimes be solved mentally which involve much larger numbers.

It certainly is well for all practical business men to be able to use readily numbers below 1,000, without recourse to written figures. In order to secure this ability, work in written arithmetic, with its own proper methods, has been deferred to a later period than usual. After practice in numbers below 1,000 has given the pupils skill in mental computation, and a clear comprehension of its principles, insight into the principles of written arithmetic will be gained much more easily.

In order that the acquired facility in mental arithmetic should be retained, it is absolutely necessary that mental arithmetic, in the narrow sense of the term, should be closely connected with written arithmetic, whether instruction in the two kinds of work is given in the same or in different hours.

Written arithmetic, as well as mental arithmetic, should not be practised mechanically, so that the operations are performed merely by rule. The shortened processes of written arithmetic should be developed out of the processes of mental arithmetic which have already been explained. If this is done, the scholar will come to know not only the processes and rules, but their reasons. The pupil is never to work by a rule, like a mathematician by his formula, till he understands the reason for his procedure and for the rule.

War is to be continually waged against all mechanical management of mathematical instruction, and against all learning of facts without reasons; yet, in the four fundamental operations of arithmetic, the pupil is to attain an ease and a rapidity of working which closely resemble that of a perfect machine; so that all his mental power may be given to the reasoning processes which the solution of the problems may require.

If the work previously suggested has been well done, the pupils are now prepared to enter upon the stage of written arithmetic proper, and readily to understand its processes.

CHAPTER V.

HIGHER NUMBERS.

36. NUMERATION.

NUMERATION properly means counting; but here it has an enlarged meaning. It signifies counting, forming higher or complex units out of a definite collection of less complex, or simple units, and also representing these different units by means of figures.

In studying numbers from 1 to 10, 1 to 20, and 1 to 1,000, the pupil has incidentally learned something of the nature of the decimal system of numbers, and of the method of representing numbers by the Arabic system of notation; but it is now time to make his knowledge more definite and systematic, and to extend it still farther. For this purpose review the grouping and writing of numbers.

Call attention to the fact that a single ball on the numeral frame, a single dot on Chart X., a single finger, etc., is represented by the figure 1 standing alone; two balls, two dots, two fingers, etc., by the figure 2; three balls, three dots, three fingers, etc., by the figure 3; and so on to nine.

Next show that a group of ten balls, ten dots, etc., is not represented by another figure, but by the figure

1 standing in the second place from the right; that two groups of ten balls, ten dots, etc., each are represented by the figure 2; three such groups by the figure 3; and so on to nine groups. Name these groups *tens*, and make the use of the name familiar by counting the rows of balls on the numeral frame, and the rows of dots on Chart X., etc., thus: one ten, two tens, three tens, etc.

Then explain that ten groups of ten each, or ten tens, are called a hundred, and are represented by the figure 1 standing in the third place; that two hundreds are represented by the figure 2; three hundreds by the figure 3; and so on to nine hundreds.

Explain that ten hundreds are called a thousand, and are represented by the figure 1 placed in the fourth place; that two thousands are represented by the figure 2; three thousands by the figure 3; and so on to nine thousands.

A good set of objects for illustrating the grouping of numbers and the use of figures may be easily made of large buttons. Single buttons are units; strings of ten each, tens; bundles of ten strings each, hundreds; packages of ten hundreds each, thousands. The figures may be written as the groups are shown.

Still another excellent apparatus for this purpose consists of ten cubes an inch on a side; nine sticks an inch square and ten inches long, marked with lines an inch apart, so as to represent inch cubes; and nine pieces of board ten inches square and an inch thick, marked off with lines an inch apart, so as to represent 100 inch cubes each. The cubes are the units; the sticks represent the tens; the pieces of board stand for the hundreds; while all, laid up in the form of a cube, represent a thousand small cubes.

Several kinds of apparatus are better than any one kind, and good apparatus may be so used as to save the teacher much labor. But, somehow, the writing of numbers should be illustrated objectively, till the pupils can readily write any numbers from 1 to 1,000, when the objects, grouped as has just been indicated, are shown them; till they can find the objects and groups of objects representing any written number from 1 to 1,000; find the number of tens and units in any number of single objects; the number of units in any number of objects grouped in tens, as strings of buttons; the number of units in any number of tens and units; the number of hundreds in any number of tens; the number of tens in any number of hundreds; the number of tens in any number of hundreds and tens; the number of hundreds, of tens, and of units in a thousand; and the number of hundreds, tens, and units, of tens and units, and of tens, in any number of thousands, hundreds, tens, and units.

When all this can be readily done with the objects themselves, the pupils should be drilled in changing written numbers into equivalent numbers with different groupings; as, for example,

1,328 = 1 thousand, 3 hundreds, 2 tens, and 8 units.
1,328 =   13   "   2   "   " 8 "
1,328 =   132 "   " 8 "
1,328 =   1,328 "

Or the following:

24,807 = 24 thousands, 8 hundreds, 0 tens, 7 units.
24,807 =   248   "   0   "   7 "
24,807 =   2,480 "   7 "
24,807 =   24,807 "

It must be made perfectly clear to the pupils that,

a. Units   are represented by the 1st figure.
   Tens   "   "   " " 2d   "
   Hundreds   "   "   " " 3d   "
   Thousands "   "   " " 4th   "

b. 10 units   = 1 ten;
    10 tens   = 1 hundred;
    10 hundreds = thousands, etc.;

so that always ten units of a lower order are equal to one unit of the next higher order.

THOUSANDS.	HUNDREDS.	TENS.	UNITS.
			1
		1	0
	1	0	0
1	0	0	0
1	3	2	8
4	8	0	7

In this scheme are first written 1, 10, 100, 1,000. Then follows the explanation that

1 ten = 10 units.
1 hundred = 10 tens = 100 units.
1 thousand = 10 hundreds = 100 tens = 1000 units.

Then should follow the writing and analysis into thousands, hundreds, tens, and units of other numbers; as, 1,328, 4,807, etc.

The writing of numbers from dictation, by the aid of this scheme, should gradually give place to the writing of dictated numbers without such aid.

If the writing and analysis of numbers below 1,000 is thoroughly mastered, it will be but little work for the teacher to make clear to the pupil the extension of the same principles to numbers above 1,000. For this purpose the scheme given above may be extended nine or ten places. These should be broken up into groups of three places each; which can readily be done by double lines, as shown above between the thousands and hundreds. The headings of the second group, or period, would be, thousands, ten-thousands, hundred-thousands; and so of the millions, billions, etc.

When this work has been well done, the pupil needs but two more suggestions:

a. To read any number, begin at the right and divide it into periods of three figures each, except the last, which may contain three, two, or one figure; read each period as though it stood alone, adding the name of the last place in the period, except in case of the last period read; as, 24,341,101,268, to be read, — twenty-four billion, three hundred forty-one million, one hundred and one thousand, two hundred sixty-eight.

b. To write any number, begin with the highest period, and fill each subsequent period, using zeros when the period is wholly or partly omitted; for example, to write twenty-four millions and seventeen, put three zeros in the thousands period, and a zero in place of the hundreds in the units period, — 24,000,017.

The directions for extending numeration so as to cover all the higher numbers are put here for the sake of completeness, and for the use of the bright pupils; but it is well to introduce the writing of large numbers gradually, as the pupils have occasion to write them. The subject of numeration is here dwelt upon so fully because it is so intimately connected with the decimal system, and because the decimal system is usually the weakest place in arithmetical teaching in this country. When the decimal system of numbers and the Arabic notation are thoroughly understood, arithmetic is half learned. Young teachers are therefore earnestly advised to advance slowly and thoroughly through the subject.

37. Addition.

In written addition it is more convenient to begin with the lowest place, that is, with the units, and to work towards the highest, thus reversing the process of mental addition. The first examples should be the addition of numbers below 1,000, because the pupils are already familiar with these numbers.

Attention should be called to the fact that 2 boys and 3 slates make neither 5 boys nor 5 slates, etc.; by which the pupils will be led to see that only like quantities can be added. This will show the reason for adding units to units, tens to tens, hundreds to hundreds, etc.; and for writing numbers, when they are to be added, so as to bring units under units, tens under tens, etc., as a matter of convenience. These explanations made, introduce an example, as the following:

<pre>
 3
88
 9
45
13
77

232
</pre>

First add the column of units. The result is 32 units; which are equal to 3 tens and 2 units. The 2 units are written under the units; and the 3 tens are added to the column of tens. The result is 23 tens, equal to 2 hundreds and 3 tens. The whole sum is thus found to be two hundreds, three tens, and two units, or 232. At first the pupil may be allowed to write the tens resulting from adding the units, with a small figure over the column of tens, as the ₃ above.

After the pupils have had considerable practice in adding numbers below 1,000, the addition of numbers above 1,000 may be introduced. The work and explanation will appear as follows:

```
  2431
  6742
   982
  3752
 97602
   785
  6742
-------
116,605
```

The column of units give 15 units = 1 ten and 5 units. Write the five units under the line in the column of units, and add the ten to the column of tens. This gives 30 tens = 3 hundreds and 0 tens. Write the 0 tens under the tens, and add the 3 hundreds to the column of hundreds. There results 46 hundreds = 4 thousands and 6 hundreds. Write the 6 hundreds under the column of hundreds, etc.

The above examples are sufficiently long for this stage of the work. Practical problems should be introduced constantly; but for this purpose it is better to depend upon a good text-book.

Experience shows that it is very easy to make mistakes in the easiest of mathematical processes, that is, in addition; so that when certainty of results is desired, it is well to perform the additions twice, once beginning at the bottom of the columns and once at the top. Or, if the columns are very long, they may be divided into two parts, the parts added separately, and then the partial results added. If the result thus reached agrees with the result of adding the entire columns at once, the result is probably right.

38. Subtraction.

The word "subtraction" means taking away. In arithmetic it signifies the process of taking one number from another, or of finding how much larger one number is than another, that is, how many more units one number contains than another. The number which is to be diminished is called the minuend; the number which is to be taken away is called the subtrahend; the number which is left, or which shows how many units the minuend is greater than the subtrahend, or how many units the subtrahend contains less than the minuend, is called the remainder or difference.

These definitions should be developed from one or two examples; as 3 from 5, 4 from 6. It would not be without profit to illustrate the terms by performing first the act of taking one number of objects from another number; as, for example, 4 boys from 6 boys; and then the act of comparing one number with another, to find the difference; as, for example, comparing 4 boys with 6 boys, to find how many more there were in one group than in the other. Whenever numbers are to be seen in new relations, the teacher cannot take too much pains to make sure that the ideas of the numbers are clear and distinct.

Write the minuend under the subtrahend, so that, as in addition, units of the same kind will stand under one another.

Problems should be given first in which each figure in the subtrahend stands for a smaller number than the corresponding figure in the minuend; as,

  976   5 units   from 6 units   = 1 unit;
−435   3 tens   "   7 tens   = 4 tens;
= 541   4 hundreds " 9 hundreds = 5 hundreds.

Therefore there remain 5 hundreds, 4 tens, and 1 unit = 541.

When the pupils have been made familiar with such examples, problems should be introduced in which one or more figures in the subtrahend stand for larger numbers than the corresponding figures in the minuend. The two following examples with their explanations will make the principles plain upon which they are to be solved.

              7 units cannot be taken from 5 units; so
  495   we separate one of the nine tens into units,
−257   which gives 10 units; and these 10 units
= 238   added to the 5 units make 15 units. From
              15 units take 7 units, and 8 units remain. Then 8 tens, which were left, minus 5 tens, leave 3 tens; and 4 hundreds − 2 hundreds = 2 hundreds. The remainder, then, is 2 hundreds, 3 tens, and 8 units = 238.

The following problem presents an additional difficulty:

  $_{9\,9\,10}$ 2 units cannot be taken from 0 units.
  1000   Since, now, there are no tens and no hun-
−732   dreds, we change 1 thousand into 10 hun-
= 268   dreds; we change 1 of these hundreds into

10 tens, and 1 ten into 10 units. There remain then in the minuend no thousands, but 9 hundreds, 9 tens, and 10 units. Then, 2 units from 10 units = 8 units; 3 tens from 9 tens = 6 tens; and 7 hundreds from 9 hundreds = 2 hundreds. So the remainder is 2 hundreds, 6 tens, 8 units = 268.

Such examples as the last two may be readily solved by the application of the principle, that if two numbers are equally increased, the difference remains the same, and by remembering that 10 units of any order is equal to 1 unit of the next higher order:

As 6 units cannot be taken from 4 units,
274 add 10 units, making 14 units; 6 units from
− 146 14 units leaves 8 units. Add 1 ten to the 4
= 128 tens, making 5 tens, which taken from 7 tens
leaves 2 tens; and 2 hundreds − 1 hundred = 1 hundred. So that the remainder is 1 hundred, 2 tens, 8 units = 128. It will be perceived that we have added 10 units to the minuend, and their equivalent, 1 ten, to the subtrahend; and, consequently, have not changed the difference. This method of explanation and practice is believed to be easier of application than the method first explained, and is therefore recommended.

Since the minuend − the subtrahend = the remainder,

   a. The minuend − the remainder = subtrahend.
   b. The subtrahend + remainder = minuend.

We can therefore prove the correctness of the work in subtraction, either by subtracting the remainder from the minuend, in which case the subtrahend is obtained, or by adding the remainder to the subtrahend, in which case we obtain the minuend. The latter proof is more practical than the former, and should be occasionally used by the pupils.

All the principles involved in subtraction can be learned by the use of small numbers; so that it is better to give the pupils much practice with these, before introducing large numbers. In the use of practical problems small numbers are much preferable; since the imagination of pupils can then be more easily appealed to when necessary.

39. Multiplication.

The meaning of the terms used in multiplication may be made clear to the pupils in the following way. Let the teacher write, in a horizontal line on the board, seven dots, and ask, "How many dots have I made?" Then let him make, under these, two rows more, and ask, "How many rows of seven dots each have I made? How many times are seven dots repeated? How many dots are there in all?"

Then let the explanation follow, while the teacher continually points to the single dots, the rows, or the whole mass. This whole process is called multiplication. The number of dots in the first row, namely 7, is the multiplicand. The number of rows, namely 3, is the multiplier. The whole number of dots, namely 21, is the product. We have repeated 7 3 times, and the result is 21.

The work on the board, as it has grown up under the hand of the teacher, will appear thus:

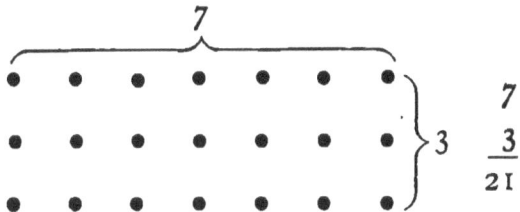

When the pupils have followed several such illustrations, they will comprehend the following definitions:

Multiplication is the process of finding how many units result from repeating a number a given number of times. The number to be repeated is called the multiplicand. The multiplier is the number showing how many repetitions are to be made. The product is the number showing how many units result from the repetitions. The multiplier and the multiplicand are called the factors of the product. Thus, in the above example, 7 is the multiplicand, 3 the multiplier, 21 the product, and 7 and 3 are the factors of 21.

It is not worth while at this stage to have these definitions committed to memory; but the terms should be thoroughly understood, so that they will bring up, in the minds of the pupils, clear and distinct ideas.

a. The examples first introduced for explanation and practice should contain two or three places in the multiplicand and only one in the multiplier. The following will show the proper explanation:

3×7 units $= 21$ units $= 2$ tens and 1 unit.
247 Write the 1 unit under the column of units.
3 3×4 tens $= 12$ tens, to which add the 2 tens
─── from the 21 units, and the sum is 14 tens $= 1$
741 hundred and 4 tens. Write the 4 tens under the tens. 3×2 hundreds $= 6$ hundreds, to which add the 1 hundred from the 14 tens, and the sum is 7 hundreds, which is to be written under the hundreds. The result is 7 hundreds, 4 tens, and 1 unit $= 741$.

b. Next follow examples with tens only in the multiplier. Here should come the explanation of the process of multiplying a number by 10. In the treatment of numbers from 1 to 1,000 it was shown that,

$10 \times 20 = 200,$ $10 \times 89 = 890,$
$10 \times 27 = 270,$ $10 \times 93 = 930,$
$10 \times 39 = 390,$ $10 \times 72 = 720,$ etc.;

in all which cases we obtained just as many tens as there were units in the multiplicand. Now since tens are indicated by a zero at their right, to multiply a number by 10 we have only to put a zero at the right, thus setting the units' figure in place of the tens', the tens' figure in place of the hundreds', etc.

Or the same may be shown by such examples as the following:

$\begin{array}{r}73\\ \times\ 10\\ \hline 730\end{array}$ 10×3 units $= 30$ units $= 3$ tens;
10×7 tens $= 70$ tens $= 7$ hundreds;
and 7 hundreds and 3 tens $= 730$.

Suppose, now, we wish to multiply a number by 40. We may first multiply by 4, and then by 10, since 10×4 times a number is 40 times the number. For example, 40×23.

$\begin{array}{r}23\\ \times\ 40\\ \hline 920\end{array}$ $4 \times 23 = 92$; $10 \times 92 = 920$.

It follows that to multiply by tens we have only to multiply by the number of tens and put a cipher after the result.

c. The third class of problems should be those with tens and units in the multiplier.

4×38 units $= 152$ units.

$\begin{array}{r}38\\ \times\ 24\\ \hline 152\\ 760\\ \hline 912\end{array}$ $\begin{array}{r}38\\ \times\ 24\\ \hline 152\\ 76\\ \hline 912\end{array}$ $20 \times 38 = 2 \times 10 \times 38 = 760 = 76$ tens; and since no units can arise from the multiplication of any number by tens, we may omit the zero as in the second example in the margin, and begin to write the product under the tens.

·Now, since 24 times a number is 4 times the number plus 20 times the number, we have only to add the partial products in order to obtain the entire product.

d. Finally, examples should be introduced with three or more figures in the multiplier; as, 243×3576.

This is equivalent to saying multiply 3,576 by 3, by 40, and by 200, and add the results.

$3 \times 3576 = 10728$, to be written units under units, etc.

$40 \times 3576 = 143040 = 14304$ tens, to be written tens under tens, etc.

$200 \times 3576 = 2 \times 100 \times 3576 = 2 \times 10 \times 10 \times 3576 = 715200 = 7152$ hundreds, to be written hundreds under hundreds, etc.

```
  3576
   243
 -----
 10728
 14304
  7152
-------
868,968
```

If, now, we add 3 times, 40 times, and 200 times the number together, we have 243 times the number.

If the pupil has observed that multiplying numbers by 10, 100, 1,000, etc., simply sets the figures one, two, three, etc., places towards the left, he at once comprehends the reason for the rule: Write the first figure of each partial product under the place of the number with which you multiply. If you multiply by units,   write the first figure under units;
" tens,   " " "   "   " tens;
" hundreds, " " " · "   " hundreds;
   etc.   · etc.

e. If the pupil thoroughly comprehends the instruction above suggested, he will have little difficulty with numbers containing ciphers.

```
   201
 × 403
 -----
   603
   804
 ------
 81,003
```

The number 201 is to be repeated 3 times; then 400 (100 × 4) times; and then the partial products are to be united.

$$\begin{array}{r} 84060 \\ \times\, 30080 \\ \hline 6724800 \\ 252180 \\ \hline 2{,}528{,}524{,}800 \end{array}$$

The number is to be repeated, first, 80 (10 × 8) times, then 30,000 (10,000 × 3) times, and the partial products added.

Such examples as the last would be introduced at this stage only for the benefit of the brightest pupils, who, by such work, may be interested and benefited.

Perhaps the easiest proof of multiplication is to make the multiplier a multiplicand and the multiplicand a multiplier, and multiply again. Later, the product may be made a dividend and the multiplicand a divisor, when the quotient should equal the multiplier.

Practical problems are to be introduced at each stage of the work of multiplication, which is here marked *a*, *b*, *c*, *d*, and *e*. For most of these, however, the teacher should depend upon a good text-book; and this should be, a part of the time, in the hands of the pupils.

40. Division.

The number to be divided is called the dividend; the number by which we divide, the divisor; the number which shows how many times the divisor is contained in the dividend, or what part of the dividend the divisor is, the quotient; the number left when the division is not completed, the remainder. For example, the process of finding how many times 7 is contained in 21, or what a seventh part of 21 is, is the division of 21 by 7. Here 21 is the dividend, 7 is the divisor, and 3 the quotient. Had we attempted to find how many times 7 is contained in 23, we should have found that it was contained 3 times, with a remainder of 2.

Whether we attempt to find how many times a number is contained in a given number, or what the corresponding part of the given number is, the process is the same; for example, take the above numbers, 21 and 7. The seventh part of 7 is 1, the seventh part of 2 times 7 is 2; and, in general, the seventh part of 21 is as many units as 7 is contained times in 21, namely 3. So that it is not necessary to consider the two kinds of division separately, although the pupil should always be required to know and to state what he is doing.

The degree of difficulty in division depends upon the constitution of the divisor; so that the divisor determines the stages of the pupils' work in division. They are the following :

 a. The divisor is composed of units ;
 b. " " " " " tens ;
 c. " " " " " tens and units ;
 d. " " contains 2, 3, etc., places.

Since, however, it is easier to make the process understood if the dividend is small, examples should be chosen for the first work where that is the case.

DIVIDING BY UNITS.

We will first explain an example of division by 2.

```
      a                    b                      c
2)759(379            2)759(300              ½ of 759
  6.. ×2               600                  ½ "  600 = 300
  ─────                ─────                ½ "  140 =  70
  15.758               159( 70              ½ "   18 =   9
  14   1               140                  ½ "    1 =   ½
  ─────                ─────                ½ of 759 = 379½
  19 759               19(  9
  18                   18 379
  ──                   ──
   1                    1
```

a. The number 759 consists of 7 hundreds, 5 tens, and 9 units. We first divide 6 hundreds by 2, and we have 3 hundreds. These 3 hundreds we write at the right. We indicate that 2 × 3 hundreds, or 6 hundreds, have been divided by writing 6 under 7. We subtract 6 hundreds from 7 hundreds, and 1 hundred remains, to which we unite the 5 tens, and have 15 tens. We divide 14 tens by 2, and the result is 7 tens, which we set in the tens' place. We write 2 × 7 tens = 14 tens under the tens to show that they have been divided. We subtract the 14 tens, and there remains 1 ten, to which we add the 9 units, and we have 19 units. We divide 18 units by 2, and obtain 9 units, which we write in the units' place in the quotient. We subtract 2 × 9 units, or 18 units, from the 19 units, and have a remainder of 1. So that the result, or product, is 371, and 1 remainder.

Under *b* the division is indicated more fully. The parts of the dividend which have been divided (600, 140, 18), as well as the parts of the quotient (300, 70, and 9), are written out in full. The third form, *c*, is the form with which the pupil is familiar in his mental work. It is added here to make the new and shortened form of division still clearer. The form *b* is recommended only for the purpose of explaining the reason of form *c*. The first form is the one to be used in practical work.

Here, more than anywhere else, is it necessary for the pupil to write the different figures in the proper places, — units under units, tens under tens, etc. To assist the teacher in securing this, the division of the board, and also the slate, into little rectangles, as formerly advised, is very helpful.

Abundant practice in dividing by 2 should precede the dividing by other units. A clear comprehension of the reason for the different parts of the process, as well as great facility in the operation, cannot be too strenuously insisted upon, before the pupil is allowed to go on to new work. Time spent here is more than saved later.

It is important that the pupil learn to determine, as soon as he begins to divide, how many places there must be in the quotient; because this explains the reason for putting a zero in the quotient, whenever the divisor is not contained in the number of units of any order in the multiplicand. An example will make this clear.

```
6)184549(30,758
  18
  ──
  45
  42
  ──
   34
   30
   ──
   49
   48
   ──
    1
```

Since 1 hundred-thousand cannot be divided by 6 and produce a whole number, we divide 18 ten-thousands by 6, and the result is 3 ten-thousands. This shows the pupil that there must be 5 places in the quotient, which the beginner may indicate by 5 points. Since 4 thousands divided by 6 produce no thousands, a zero must be put in the quotient in the thousands' place; else the quotient would not contain 5 places, and the first figure, 3, would be read 3 thousands; for 4 thousands and 5 hundreds, or 45 hundreds, divided by 6, give 7 hundreds. By such examples the pupil will learn to put a zero in the quotient whenever the number shown by bringing down a figure of the dividend is not divisible by the divisor.

The correctness of the work in division may be tested by multiplying the divisor by the quotient, and adding the remainder to the product. The sum should equal the dividend.

After the pupils have had a good deal of practice in dividing by numbers represented by one figure, using the form given above, they may be allowed to divide by the same numbers, writing simply the divisor under the dividend, thus:

$$2 \overline{\smash{)}9^15^17^12\,6\,1}$$
$$\overline{4\ 7\ 8\ 6\ 3\ 0} - 1 \text{ remainder.}$$

At first the remainder may be written in small figures over and a little at the left of the next place.

DIVIDING BY TENS.

It is well to make a distinct step of dividing by numbers consisting of tens only, because it throws light on the succeeding steps in division. It would be profitable, at this point, to review the mental processes of multiplying, and also of dividing, by 10, 20, 30, etc., to 100. This done, an example or two will make this step understood.

```
20)4165(208
    40
   ---
    165
    160
    ---
      5
```

The twentieth of 41 hundreds is 2 hundreds, and a remainder of 1 hundred; to this 1 hundred, or 10 tens, add 6 tens, and the sum is 16 tens; which is not divisible by 20, and so there are no tens in the quotient, and the tens' place must be filled with a zero. Dividing 165 units by 20, and we have 8 units, with a remainder of 5.

It will soon be obvious to the pupils that dividing by 10 is accomplished by cutting off the unit figure, and regarding it as representing tenths; and so, later, of dividing by 100, 1,000, etc.

DIVISION.

DIVIDING BY NUMBERS OF TWO PLACES.

The difficulty of dividing by such numbers arises from the fact that the pupils do not know the multiplication table for numbers so large; and hence the products of these numbers, that is, the divisors used, must be found. For this purpose it is often necessary for the pupils at first to proceed by way of trial. This trial consists in finding how often a convenient number of about the same size as the divisor — that is, a number whose product by 2, 3, 4, etc., to 9, is already known — is contained in the number to be divided, and then multiplying the divisor by this quotient. For example, if I wish to find how many times 53 is contained in 480, I first see how often 50 is contained in it. This I know by knowing the products of the tens, that is, 20, 30, etc., by 2, 3, etc. Since 50 is contained 9 times in 480, therefore it is probable that 53 is contained 9 times; this is here the fact, for $9 \times 53 = 477$. Here the probability and the truth agree; but were the divisor 54, this would not be the case; for $9 \times 54 = 486$. In this case the quotient must be diminished by 1. The nearer the convenient number, or trial divisor, is to the true divisor, the greater the probability is that the trial quotient will prove to be the true quotient. Hence in dividing by 56, 57, 58, or 59, it would be better to use 60, rather than 50, as a trial divisor, while 50 would be more likely than 60 to give us the true number, if we were dividing by 50, 51, 52, 53, or 54. In the former case it would often be necessary to increase the trial quotient by 1 in order to obtain the true quotient.

After much experience, and practice, the pupil can make this trial in his mind without writing down any of the work; and this power the teacher should try to develop in the pupil.

The following is a typical explanation : 7 hundreds ÷ 23 gives no hundreds; 7 hundreds + 5 tens = 75 tens; 75 tens ÷ 23 = 3 tens, for 3 × 23 tens = 69 tens. There remain 6 tens, to which add 1 unit, and we have 61 units. 61 units ÷ 20 = 3; but 3 × 23 = 69; so 23 is not contained in 61 units 3 times, but one less than 3 times, or 2 times; 2 × 23 = 46; and 61 − 46 = 15, the remainder.

```
23)751(32
    69
    ―――
    61
    46
    ―――
    15
```

```
9254)78632594(
     74032
     ―――――
     46005
     37016
     ―――――
     89899
     83286
     ―――――
      66134
      64778
      ―――――
       1356
```

```
      8497
    × 9254
    ―――――
    33988
    42485
    16994
    76473
    ―――――――
    78631238
        1356
    ―――――――
    78632594
```

7 ten-millions are not divisible by 9254;
78 millions are not divisible by 9254;
786 hundred-thousands are not divisible by 9254;

7863 ten-thousands are not divisible by 9254;

78632 thousands ÷ 9254 = 8000; 8000 × 9254 = 74032 thousands, which taken from 78632 thousands leave 4600 thousands = 46000 hundreds, to which add 5 hundreds, and we have 46005 hundreds; 46005 hundreds ÷ 9254 = 400; 400 × 9254 = 37016 hundreds, which subtracted from 46005 hundreds leaves 8989 hundreds = 89890 tens, to which add 9 tens, and the sum is 89899 tens; 89899 tens ÷ 9254 = 90; 90 × 9254 = 83286 tens, which taken from 89899 tens leave 6613 tens = 66130 units, to which add 4 units, and we have 66134 units; 66134 units ÷ 9254 = 7; 7 × 9254 = 64778, which from 66134 = 1356, remainder.

Of course examples of this length would be given only to older and brighter pupils.

The pupil can now prove his multiplication by dividing the product either by the multiplier or the quotient. If the work is right, the quotient will be the other factor.

www.ingramcontent.com/pod-product-compliance
Lightning Source LLC
Chambersburg PA
CBHW030244170426
43202CB00009B/625